SUN SIGN SECRETS

Sun Sign Secrets

The ultimate astrological guide to yourself

Bernard Fitzwalter

This edition publish 1993 by
Diamond Books
77–85 Fulham Palace Road,
Hammersmith, London W6 8JB

First published in twelve volumes by
The Aquarian Press 1989
This compilation 1991

Printed in Great Britain by
HarperCollinsManufacturing Glasgow

CONTENTS

INTRODUCTION

People love finding out about themselves through astrology, and the two questions which are asked most frequently are 'What am I like?' and 'Who is best suited to me?' This little book will answer both of those questions, and it will answer a lot more as well. It will identify not only the person best suited to you, but also the person you are most likely to disagree with — and every possible variation in between.

And there's more. Most people are obsessed with their appearance, but few have any idea that their zodiac sign has any bearing on the way they look. It has, and here's a special guide to help you match the signs to physique. Cars . . . holidays . . . favourite food . . . The list goes on and on, yet the zodiac touches all of these and more, making everything reflect your birthday. It's all laid out here for you, along with everything else you could want to know about *your* sign, from the famous people born under it to the myth which lies behind it.

Dip in, and get to know yourself!

Bernard Fitzwalter

1
THE TWELVE SIGNS

BEING AN ARIES

Bright, dashing, energetic, sporty — that's what Arians are like. First sign of the zodiac, first to have a go, and usually first to finish, Arians are never happier than when they have something to do. Your guiding planet, Mars, keeps you full of vitality, and no sooner have you thought of something than you are off doing it. It's far too hasty an approach for most of us — but Arians get away with it every time.

This boundless energy needs something to keep itself occupied with, and you're always bursting to get started on the next job. Very capable and very fit, you always assume that everybody is at least as enthusiastic as you are, and although you would never ask anybody to do anything you couldn't do yourself, it sometimes surprises you that other people don't have your capabilities.

An Arian lives in, and through, his body. It sounds obvious, but not all of us do; Geminis and Sagittarians live through their imagination, while Cancerians live through their emotions. An Arian lives through his body. Simply being inside such a marvellous vehicle gives you a feeling of well-being that people from other signs simply don't have; that's why you like to be on your feet and doing things all the time, because the more active you are, the better you feel. Conversely, of course, when you are ill for any reason, you feel utterly

The typical Aries!

desolate, because the thing you value most — your body — isn't working properly. Fortunately, this doesn't happen very often; you have more than enough natural vitality to combat most of the minor ailments that the rest of us get. The only minor ailment which might afflict you regularly is a headache, which you get when your natural energy is held in by difficult circumstances. In other words, when things get too tough, you try harder and harder, but when things are absolutely impossible and you can't make headway at all, you get headaches. Other Sun signs would give up and do something else, but you just keep slogging away at things until you get what you want from them. That's Arian directness and strength for you, but a little flexibility from time to time wouldn't go amiss.

Because you are at your best when you are active, you like to get working on anything new as soon as you can. Thinking about it and considering the best approach seems like a waste of time to you — you'd rather be getting on with it. You have so much confidence in your own abilities that it never occurs to you that you could ever fail, and it is true, to a certain extent; you attack problems with such energy and determination that most of them melt away, though it is interesting to speculate on how many of them wouldn't have occurred in the first place if you had spent a little time thinking about things beforehand.

Emotionally, you are very straightforward. You either like things, or you don't, and you are just the same with people. Like the other Fire signs — Leo and Sagittarius — you lack subtlety: if you want something (or somebody) you go for it, and if not you have no time for it at all. It is a constant surprise to you when you discover that somebody has lied to you, or that something is not quite what it seems; in your world everything is clear-cut, black and white, and real enough to touch. When you meet deception and disappointment you are very upset, like a child who has had toys taken away for no reason; you are suddenly confronted with a world where physical activity is of no use, and you don't know what to do. Your friends would do well to remember that although you enjoy rough-and-tumble fun and games, you are very upset by tricks and deceit.

Luckily, you have a very short memory. Aries is the sign of the immediate present: what interests you is what is happening right now, and once you have something which takes your attention, all thought of the past just vanishes. You are not working towards some far future like the Capricorn, either, where all the efforts of today will be rewarded; you are being active here and now because that's all that matters to you. This short memory is most useful when you have been hurt or defeated in some way: unlike other people who would think twice before doing the same thing again, you get back up and give it another go, usually successfully the second time round.

You make a wonderful friend — strong, honest, and uncomplicated. Whenever there's a worthy cause that needs extra manpower, or someone who knows what needs to be done but lacks the ability to put it into effect, then you're there alongside with your sleeves rolled up, happily helping out. Doing a simple job with strength and willing, is what you're best at, in many ways. Anybody who needs a friend to understand their problems, though, or to be around as a shoulder to cry on, shouldn't choose you because that's not the sort of friend you are. Nor do they need you if they are the sort of people who cry about one thing but are actually upset about something completely different: you're too straightforward to see what they really mean, and although you're willing to sympathize with anyone who is upset, you're uneasy in complex emotional situations. There are also those who seem unable to function without someone else as a support, and, though not unusual, it does seem odd to you. You like people who can stand on their own feet and are so busy with their own activities that they don't really have time to sit and worry — just like yourself, in fact.

Arians in love are strong, direct, and very physical. You know what you want, and you know love makes you feel good, and you just want more of it — a typically straightforward Arian response. When you fall in love, it's with an all-consuming passion, a direct and uncomplicated desire to be with someone forever. Your passion is there for all to see; it's not in your nature to hide your feelings, and you can't see the advantages of secret liaisons or a love which mustn't be shown. That sort of thing strikes you as either slightly soppy, or downright weird: in your way of doing things you either want somebody or you don't — and if you do you do something about it in the most effective and positive manner. It never even occurs to you to consider what other people might think or do; what matters to you is the passion of the moment, the passion which drives you. As with all things in your life, though, that initial passion has to be kept up if you are not to lose interest, and that's difficult with a personal relationship. As months turn into years, personal relationships become static and settled, and that's just the sort of thing that you don't like. If there's no movement, no challenge, you lose interest — and you start to look around for somebody else. It's a real problem, and not helped by the fact that you are often happiest on your own. You're just not the settling type; you're an explorer, and to go where you've been before seems dull.

BEING A TAURUS

Kind, caring, unhurried, dependable: these are the words which spring to mind when trying to describe a Taurean friend to somebody who has never met one.

The typical Taurus!

Everybody needs a Taurean in their life somewhere: they are the ones you can rely on, the ones who are loyal and unchanging. They are also the ones who refuse to move from what they see as their territory, and whose stubbornness will have anybody else close to tears: a Taurean just won't budge.

Taureans are like the bull which is the animal of the sign. Bulls are usually in a field on their own; they don't roam around it much, but nobody is in any doubt whose field it is, and most people would rather walk round it than cross it uninvited. You Taureans have a very strong sense of what's yours, and you like the familiar feel of them; they remind you who you are. It is as if your identity was somehow contained in your surroundings, and if other people treat your things without due respect, it is as if they were walking over your face. It is very difficult for them to understand this, and it is equally difficult for you to understand that other people don't have the same affection for their home and their possessions.

There is a wonderful sense of quiet, steady care which seems to radiate from Taureans. You seem to want to look after things, to keep them safe and secure. In your perfect world, everything would be warm and well-fed, and nothing would ever change or go away. A lot of people appreciate this quality in you; when things go wrong, or events start moving too quickly and people start to get hurt, the soothing comfort that Taureans offer is the best thing in the world. Of course, when things are going well, and life looks full of new and exciting things, then Taurus looks slow and uninteresting, but you can't be everything to everybody all of the time.

It's not that Taureans won't move quickly, it's just that they'd rather not. You know what I mean: you'll move when you have had time to make your mind up, and that takes careful consideration. For the most part, you tend to find that things are better the way they were,

and you won't move this time, thank you. Taurean
captains go down with their ship because they are used
to being on board, and because the lifeboats look a bit
flimsy and insubstantial in comparison; they'd rather
stay with what they are familiar with.

When you do move, it is usually because somebody
has pushed you beyond your limits. You have an
almost unlimited capacity for punishment, but only
almost. When you have taken more than even you can
stand, then you move. The process is very similar to the
charging bull in the field; there is plenty of warning, but
when it happens it is still pretty frightening. There is
also the problem, from the Taurean point of view, that
you tend to have your eyes shut when you charge, just
like the bull; you can do a lot of damage that way. On
the odd occasions when you try to get things done in a
temper, you cause havoc. This is usually referred to as
being like a bull in a china shop. It sounds corny, but
it's true — every phrase in the language which
describes the actions of a bull can be applied to a
Taurean.

There is more to being Taurean than being caring,
being conservative, and having a touchy temper. The
essence of Taurean thought is *keeping your own things
as they are*. This is why you are resistant to change,
why you care for anything which is hurt or damaged,
and why you are very sensitive about what is yours.
The emphasis on the quality of things also gives you a
very special talent: you have taste. You have taste in
food, for example. Taureans are usually very good
cooks (indeed, many chefs are Taurean), and you know
what you're looking for when you're out buying your
meat and veg. You have taste in fabrics, too, your eye
for cut and line, and especially your eye for colour, are
better than that of any other sign, except possibly Libra.
Even then, Libra doesn't have your appreciation of the
feel of the fabric. Finally, you have taste in music. You
may not know much musical theory, but you have a

good ear, and most probably a good voice, too. In fact, anything involving taste or touch, in any senses of the words, is a Taurean activity. You have a very broad talent indeed.

Physical reassurance is very important to a Taurean, and it comes in a variety of forms. You may notice how fond you are of your food, for instance. What you are doing is making sure that you get enough, and that you're not likely to starve to death. It sounds funny, I know, but Taureans are like that — they need to know that their bodies are being looked after. It reassures them. Taureans like their food to be of the highest quality, too. Your body deserves the best, in your opinion. A tremendous number of Taureans, men as well as women, either own, or work in, restaurants, and those that don't are the sort who develop formidable home cooking repertoires. If a Taurus has friends round to his place to eat (and he will do, because that way he stays in the place where he feels most secure) they will not be getting beans on toast, I can assure you.

Physical reassurance means body contact, too, and Taureans are big on hugs and strokes. Your conversation may be a bit slow, but your touch speaks volumes, and other people should learn to listen to it, because it's how you communicate best. If your partner likes you to demonstrate your affections by holding him, then he should be in heaven in your arms, but if he wants sharp wit or flamboyant gestures as well, then perhaps he's got the wrong person. You're soft, quiet and sensuous.

Reassurance and security go hand in hand, of course, and following on from them come familiarity and solidity. This is the downside of Taurus — your unwillingness to give up or change your position. People will try to get you to change your mind, but their words run off you like rain. They try and get you to change your position, but you won't budge. The same goes for your emotional ties, too. As far as you're concerned, once you're with someone, you stay with them. You can be insulted, threatened, attacked, and even wounded, but you won't move. You may bleed to death emotionally, or die of a broken heart when he finally leaves you, but you won't give up. Not ever. You quite simply don't know how to.

So what is a Taurean? A gardener, basically. You look after your patch carefully, and you make it produce colour and beauty in a way that seems beyond the rest of us. If it can be done with care and patience, a Taurean can do it to perfection. The pity is that other people occasionally trample on the flowers, and you get very understandably cross.

BEING A GEMINI

Variety — that's the Gemini motto. Never willing to stay with one thing for long, the Gemini wants up-to-the-minute information about *everything*. To you, the world is full of people talking to each other, and you want to be part of every conversation. Conferencing, telephones, multi-screen video, and round-the-clock new ideas; gruesome for most people, but paradise for a Gemini.

The essence of the Gemini are the thoughts in your head. For some signs, like Aries and Sagittarius, the important thing in life is to be active; for others, such as Cancer and Pisces, the important thing is to be sympathetic and sensitive. For a Gemini, the important thing is to think and talk.

Geminis need to feed their minds; you get hungry for new ideas and new experiences, and above all for new people to talk to. You are insatiably curious: you love to see and hear about new things, and you like to turn a new idea this way and that in your imagination, to see what it has to offer you. You do the same with words,

The typical Gemini!

too, twisting what people say to see if it sounds any better another way round. It's a bit like shaking a present that you're not allowed to unwrap to see if it makes any noises and gives you any clues.

One of the things that the other eleven signs have difficulty with is just how fast your mind works. You are so quick on the uptake that you have taken the idea on board before they have finished the sentence; if they have another sentence to add which says essentially the same thing then you are likely to try and turn it round or alter its meaning in your response, just for something to do, because you have become bored already — in a matter of seconds. It is a full time job for you to keep your mind supplied with new things, and if you have the sort of job where you don't see a lot of people, then you will have difficulties keeping yourself amused. You probably recognize the problem already and keep yourself busy with books, magazines, and puzzles; they're no substitute for real conversation, though, as you know very well.

It is often said that Geminis are schizophrenic, simply because the constellation for their sign has two people in it. Whilst this is obviously not true, you are certainly changeable in outlook and are quite capable of being happy in the morning and depressed in the afternoon. The reason is again to do with the time scale on which you function. Like a toddler, you work on a scale in which a quarter of an hour is quite a long time, and an afternoon is an eternity. You can run through every emotion you have, and completely change your feelings about something, in a few minutes.

Even the way that you think is different from the other eleven signs. What you do is to compare one thing to another and notice the difference between them. Most people go through life trying to make connections between things which are similar — the process of recognition, if you think about it — but not you. You like things to be different. You even produce different

versions of the same phrase in your head and compare
them to see if they make a different sort of sense. The
only snag is that you do all this with the volume turned
up, so that other people think that what you say is what
you mean. It isn't at all — what you say is what
happened to be passing through your mind at that
particular moment.

Geminis have an entirely undeserved reputation for
being cheats and liars; again, it is all to do with the way
your mind works. If you turn a phrase round to mean
the opposite, your intention is to amuse yourself, not to
deceive anyone else. If you can play a game of cards
such that the points go one way but the advantage goes
another, that's not cheating, that's playing on two
different levels at once. It all boils down to the same
thing — you're making sure that whatever you are
doing offers your mind a variety of things to deal with at
once.

There are a lot of things Geminis can do that the rest
of us can't, or not as easily. For a start, you can read
anything. That doesn't sound too difficult, but what
about reading music, or reading shorthand, or reading
a foreign language, or a foreign script, such as Russian?
For most of us that's more than our brains will easily
take, but for a Gemini it's just another opportunity to
think on more than one level at the same time. For you
it's easy and it's fun. What this means, of course, is that
if you're idling your time away with word puzzles and
the crossword, then *don't*; use that Gemini talent for
languages and reading to learn something worthwhile
instead, like Chinese!

Spare time is a problem for you. Most people are
only too willing to sit still and do nothing, but not you —
you get fidgety and start looking round for something to
do. You are quite capable of reading the paper and
watching television at the same time. You probably
phone your friends while you are doing both of these; it
helps to keep your mind busy.

Geminis have tremendous talents. You are bright, clever, sharp, good talkers, and you are *fast*. What you are not, however, is sentimental or emotionally sensitive. There's a reason for this and it has to do with two things, astrologically. The first is that Gemini is an Air sign, and the second is that Gemini is one of the signs of the planet Mercury.

Air signs are the ones where the most important things are words and ideas. Where other people are concerned, it's not how close you feel to each other which matters, or how much you trust and rely on each other, but what you have to say to each other that matters. A Gemini is always interested in what another person has to say, or what their ideas are. It doesn't matter whether you agree with them or not — it's just your curiosity and love of novelty which makes you want to know what they think, so that you can compare it to what's going on inside *your* head. You probably won't take up their point of view, but that's not important; you're only doing it to give yourself something to think about. All the Air signs work this way: the focus is on the exchange of words, not on anything else.

Mercury is the smallest planet which in astrology looks after everything which is either intellectual, fast-moving, or both. Assigned to Gemini, it shows how quickly your mind works, and also how it likes to move on to the next thing, never staying in one place for more than a moment. Emotionally, however, Mercury is cold; it can't show feelings, only thoughts.

Emotions and sentiment are to do with Water in astrology, not with Air, and both of them grow through spending time with something or somebody, which is just what you never do. Air needs to keep moving, and Mercury needs to keep thinking, so between them they keep Gemini on the go, never settling.

You need variety; it's as simple as that. As long as there are new things to see and to talk about, and new people to meet, you're going to want to see them and talk to them. It's what you were made for.

BEING A CANCER

Moody? Shy? Withdrawn? Sensitive? Touchy, even? All of these are words which are applied to Cancerians, and it must upset you when you hear yourself referred to in this way. Somehow all your positive qualities pass unnoticed, and that hurts, because deep down you care about things, and not just about yourself. You care about other people far more than they will ever know — and far more than you will ever let them!

What makes you the person you are is your emotional state. It seems like an obvious statement to make, but only Scorpios and Pisceans work in anything like a similar way to you — the other nine signs can't see what you're making such a fuss about. What matters to you above all is happiness and safety, both for yourself and for those close to you, and your efforts to ensure this are what determines your life. Needless to say, making sure that you are always safe and secure is a worrying business, and you do worry about it; most Cancerians can be seen frowning from the effort of looking after themselves. Relax your face. Doesn't that feel better? Has the sky fallen in yet? I know what you're going to say; you're going to say that it *might* do, and soon.

Cancerians care very deeply about their family and close friends. Once you have made a friend of somebody, they are there for ever. *They* may not know it, but you do. You celebrate their successes; you commiserate with their reverses. You cry at their weddings; you go round to look after them when they are ill. It's all part of something that Cancerians do better than anybody else — caring.

Some of this caring is expressed in a protective way.

The typical Cancer!

When one of your family or friends is hurt or threatened, you will fight on their behalf, stick up for them, make complaints, and generally get hostile. Anybody who thinks that Cancerians are shy and withdrawn has never seen one defend a friend. No matter who the enemy is, they'll wish they hadn't started when they attack the friend of a Cancerian. She will take on employers, local councils, whole Governments — size doesn't enter into it.

You can defend yourself, too, though an Arian wouldn't call it much of a defence, because he defends by attacking. You defend by defending, which is how things should be. Think of the crab of the sign. Crabs back themselves into secure little holes under rocks and places like that. Any creature that comes near has to deal with the pincers before it can tackle the problem of the crab's position, and even then there's its shell to consider. That's quite a firm defence system, and Cancerian people work in exactly the same way. When threatened, you retreat into a safe position; if the threat continues, you snap your pincers. This is when everybody says that you are touchy. At this stage you will tell yourself off for being over-sensitive to what was probably a bit of fun, and decide to let things pass over you. You retire into yourself a little, get on with your own business, and tell yourself that there's no need to get involved or react to what's going on around you. Now everybody says you're being moody.

When real trouble occurs, you defend your position with real tenacity. It is very difficult to get you to give up what's yours, except when the situation is genuinely hopeless. Even then, you won't retreat — you prefer to move to one side and let the problem go by. Crabs are famous for walking sideways, you will recall.

Your outer shell is easy to see, but few people understand what's inside it. That's how you like it, for the most part, and the only people allowed to get close enough to find out are those whom you trust completely. Inside that shell is a very emotional creature indeed. The sign Cancer is governed by the Moon, and you will find that your emotions go in phases, too. Not only will you react to the Moon's monthly cycles, but you will react to many smaller cycles, too. You are extremely sensitive to what is said to you, or what opinion people hold of you: you can hide your reaction behind your shell, but the reaction is there none the less, and you won't forget a deep insult in a hurry. Anyone who goes out of his way to be kind to you will have his kindness repaid many times over in years to come, but anyone who makes you feel silly or who hurts you with his tactless remarks will never be forgiven, and his words will be in your mind every time you see him.

It is this very sensitivity which makes you able to understand the needs of others when they are depressed or uncertain — it is the root of your capacity for care. The comfort and understanding they need is what you are able to provide, because you are as sensitive to their condition as you are to your own. Oddly enough, your feelings about yourself lead you to be withdrawn and defensive, but as soon as you find somebody who needs your care your own troubles cease to concern you. Their needs become more important and all your energies are given to their protection and welfare.

You may be over-sensitive, you may be cautious and withdrawn, but the care and support you give to the rest of us when we are down is worth far, far more.

And yet, despite all this care and consideration, Cancerians are far more successful and assertive than a lot of people, especially you Cancerians yourselves, would credit. You're actually quite good at making the first move, at doing what has to be done, and at staying with something for as long as is necessary to see it through to completion. It may be that you do things on your own because you worry that anybody else might not know what they were doing, and that they might make a mess of it, and it is almost certainly the case that you stay with things for as long as is necessary because you can't stand the worry of not knowing whether it's all going to work out the way it should, but at least things get completed that way. The end result is that in a work environment, provided that the way forward is reasonably clear-cut, you are likely to be successful, simply because you work steadily and conscientiously, and you care about what you're doing.

A lot of people make the mistake of thinking that because you don't show a great deal of emotion when you're in public, that you're equally cool in your personal life. Nothing could be further from the truth. Strong emotion is the centre of your existence; it's the stuff you are made of. What you want out of a relationship is complete mutual trust, so that all your emotional energy can be shared and enjoyed without having to be defensive or worried. It sounds wonderful, and it is, but the other eleven signs hardly know it's there because most of them think that what's on the outside must be what's on the inside, too. All they see is someone who doesn't say much, and who worries about things in case they go wrong. Cancer, you are the great hidden treasure of the zodiac.

BEING A LEO

Leo isn't just a star sign — it's *the* star sign, the sign of the stars. Every Leo knows that they are the star of the show, the centre of attention, the natural number one. When you look at the glitterati arriving for the Oscar awards in their limousines, you know that it is only a matter of time before you take your rightful place amongst them; the idea that you might not make it to the very top never even enters your head.

Leo is at the centre of the zodiac in the same way that

The typical Leo!

the Sun is at the centre of the solar system, and being a
Leo gives you all the qualities of the Sun: you are warm,
radiant, and loved by almost everybody. You can light
up a room by being in it, in the same way that the Sun
can light up a dull day by coming out from the clouds.
Any party is a better party when the Leo arrives —
things are somehow dull without you!

Leos are natural winners, and you get that way
through an interesting blend of selfishness and
generosity. It works as follows: you know that you are
quite simply the best person imaginable. Self-doubt,
self-criticism, shyness, and reticence were all left out of
the recipe somewhere when you were made — they
simply do not occur in the sign of Leo. If you are as
good as you know you are, therefore, you must know
best what's good for you. Nobody else is as important
as you, and nobody else can possibly know as well as
you what your needs are, so you feel quite justified in
pleasing yourself. This means that you get your own
way the whole time, and you continue to feel pleased
with yourself, because you don't have to do things that
you don't want to.

In any other sign of the zodiac that attitude would
produce an unbearably selfish egotist, and yet
everybody likes Leos for precisely those qualities:
why? Because you are genuine, and because you are
generous. What you've got you are quite willing to
share, provided that you are appreciated for it. You
enjoy showing off, basically: you think that you are so
good that the world ought to see it. You're right — you
are that good, and the world loves to see it. By being
with you the rest of the world gets to have a good time
and can share in your glory. They don't know how to
organize themselves: they lack your confidence and
sense of what's best. So, you show them what's best,
which is of course *your* way of doing things, and they
thank you for it. They feel successful, and you feel
appreciated: everybody wins.

You're not trying to trick anybody, or to put them down. You don't need to: as far as you're concerned you're at the top anyway, and everyone else is less. Your confidence means that you have no fear for your position, nor jealousy of anyone else's success: good for them, you say, and it doesn't alter your own opinion of yourself one bit. That may sound pompous, and maybe it is, but it means that when you offer your opinions and help to others, they don't have to wonder what you get out of it. Your generosity and optimism isn't something you use as a means to an end, it's given away for free.

That's why you're so popular. Genuine cheeriness and optimism, available for free. It may not seem much to you, but if you could see through the eyes of the other eleven signs you would realize what a rare commodity it really is. We can come to you full of doubt and gloom, and you will tell us what we ought to be doing. What's more, you will invite us to share in the good times that you have made for yourelf, and you will be ready to appreciate what little progress we have managed to make on our own. You give us warmth and hope: all we have to do in return is tell you how good you are. We get the good side of that deal, believe me, Leos.

You have other talents, too, besides being warm, radiant, and generous. You are terrific organizers: you know what you're doing, and it's easy from there to see what everybody else should be doing as well. The rest of us can't see things so clearly, I'm afraid. You encourage the efforts of the rest of us without being critical, and you are more than willing to take up positions of leadership when the rest of us doubt our capabilities. Kings, chairmen, governors, leaders of all kinds: they all require Leonine qualities, and it is much easier to be one than to become one.

There are drawbacks, of course, though they are invisible to you. We forgive you your excesses because we get so much joy from being with you that we can overlook the minor irritations. You have a habit of expecting things to be done for you, for one thing; I'm sure this is normal for one in your position, your majesty, but it can surprise and annoy us lesser beings. You take a dim view, too, of things which mock your high position, as the last sentence did: kings have dignity, after all.

Something else that may seem like a drawback to everyone else, but not necessarily to you, is that you may not be able to find, or even want, somebody who is able to match your brilliance and warmth to the extent required in a life partnership. Most people spend their time trying to find that special person who can supply all the qualities they lack, and provide warmth, support, or whatever. Leos don't need that: you have so much energy yourself that you can afford to give it out to everyone else, and you are quite likely to be happy on your own, provided that you have enough people around you. What you need is to be appreciated; you radiate your warmth at people, and they reflect it back to you. The more people you have around you, obviously, the better the system works, and this is what makes Leos such fun to be with; you can turn any occasion into party time simply by acting as a focus for the activity and projecting your personality onto the crowd. It's a great talent, and one which wins you a lot of friends.

There are only two things which really bother you. The first is when somebody threatens to take over your role in life. If anybody is going to be warm, generous and appreciated it is going to be you, as far as you are concerned, and you won't stand for competition. You will either fight them strongly, or, if they look like winning, you will retire with as much dignity as you can muster, and go somewhere where you will be appreciated as you were before. The second thing which bothers you is when events change around you, threatening your settled way of life. You like things to stay more or less the way you have arranged them, and changing circumstances threaten loss of dignity: it's worrying for you.

Apart from that, about the only thing which is ever troublesome for you is lack of funds to live life on the level you feel you deserve. Leos instinctively recognize the best of everything, and you know how to appreciate and enjoy it. Anything else is less — but sometimes it's all you can afford. Despite that, Leos do seem to enjoy a higher lifestyle than the other signs: whether you earn more, or just enjoy it instead of saving is difficult to say.

Unwilling to change, slightly lazy and a little pompous; but mostly, Leo, you are just what we all need, and life would be a darker and colder place without you.

BEING A VIRGO

Virgos are selfless people who will do anything to help anybody else. They are painstaking and neat; they are usually cleaner, healthier, and tidier than the rest of us; and they are patient. Yet they have possibly the worst reputation of the whole zodiac. Almost everybody has a pet Virgo they love to hate. Almost everybody sees them as harsh critics, too quick to see the faults in someone and not quick enough to praise. Their efforts to help, though readily accepted, gain scant thanks. Altogether a curious state of affairs; how does it come about?

All the characteristics of the Virgo character come from the same source; the planet Mercury. Mercury is small, quick and clever, but short of bulk and weight, and rather dry emotionally. Mercury's people, such as Virgos, tend to be the same way. You have a wonderful eye for detail; Mercury's quick and clever qualities make your mind very perceptive and observant. You are keen to learn how things work, how they should be

The typical Virgo!

done, and the best way to do them. Then you practise until you have mastered the skills necessary to do whatever you have to do — perfectly.

It takes patience to learn how to do things well, but you have plenty of that, because to you the end result is worth it. You have to understand how things are supposed to be done before you can do them for yourself. Some people can muddle through with half an idea, never bothering to ask any questions or find out what there is to know, but not you.

Once you have learned how to do something, you would like to use that skill to help others, to show them, in a way, what it is that you have understood. Most people take this the wrong way, and it is here that the poor reputation of the Virgo has its origin. When you show somebody what they are not doing right, they take it as criticism not as help. When you offer to do something for somebody, they take it as an indication that you think them incompetent, not as a desire to be of service. The reasons for this lie with them, not with you. The other eleven signs are not, for the most part, much interested in the idea of doing something for somebody else, for free: they are too selfish. As a consequence of this, they cannot understand your desire to help, and come to the conclusion that you are either showing off, or criticizing their inabilities. The reason that they are bothered about getting things wrong has something to do with the sort of education that we all had, and the fact that it was always considered a bit creepy to get things right all the time, never to be late, always to be tidy and organized — and those who were none of these things (the Pisceans) all grew up to work in the Media and perpetuate the myth that tidy and punctual Virgos were hateful creatures. Absurd, really.

There are, however, two sides to every argument, and for your part you will have to try and take into account the power of emotion in others. Just because you are ruled by a planet which is emotionally cool doesn't mean that everybody else is; in fact, only four signs put logic before feeling (the others being Gemini, Capricorn and Aquarius), and the other eight let their heart rule their head. Remember this.

Your eye for detail can have another side to it, too. To you, small things are big; little details matter. This is, of course, how you get your reputation for being fussy and nitpicking — you can see the things that other people miss. What *you miss* though, is what they can all see quite easily — the larger picture. You have a tendency to concentrate on details without looking at the larger context, and that can be quite a problem for you sometimes.

On a lighter note, all Virgos worry about their health. The idea behind it is the very Virgoan one of looking after yourself in the right and proper way, but sometimes you will take it to extremes. If there is a health food shop near you, or a pharmacist, then you will be a familiar figure to the proprietors of both; you seem to enjoy vitamins and medicines in equal amounts. If this makes your colleagues smile, then you smile too; telling them how they ought to be taking mineral supplements too will only reinforce their worst fears about Virgos.

Virgos often have quite a difficult time with their personal relationships, and it's not hard to see how this state of affairs comes about. As with everything else that you have an interest in, you are concerned to make it better, and to improve it if possible. You approach people in the same way, as you know, and so when you find someone you really care for, you show how much you care by trying to make things better for them, and trying to iron out all the imperfections in them. It doesn't occur to you that they probably like themselves the way they are, and it isn't that you're dissatisfied with them in any way — at least, not to begin with. What you want is for the world to see how absolutely *perfect* your partner is, and that's why you keep trying to remove any rough edges from them. You want them to be the way *you'd* like to be, and that's why you do it.

When this sort of caring gets too much for your partner, they tell you not to criticize, and then you're hurt. What has happened is that they have misunderstood your intentions, and you somehow feel that it must be because you haven't been doing things properly, so you try again. This can produce a vicious circle at times — the harder you try, the more you are rebuffed.

A second problem area with Virgoan relationships is your relatively low emotional level. Virgos are so hardworking, and so sensible that it never occurs to them that other people can virtually change their character, and certainly change their likes and dislikes, according to their mood. A partner who is one way one day, and completely different the next, confuses you, and you tend to steer away from that sort of thing altogether. In doing so, of course, you are ignoring what is likely to be the core of the relationship for the other person, and preventing yourself from ever becoming familiar with it — which is another vicious circle. Relationships are made out of compromised differences, and compromise isn't one of your strongest points. The more you can learn to do it, the easier your relationships become.

You have a great deal to offer, but it must be presented very carefully, and that's not easy. Showing how perceptive you are without seeming nosy, being shrewd without being shrewish, is a constant struggle for Virgos. Never mind — Taureans and Capricorns appreciate you, and Cancerians and Scorpios actually like you, so that can't be bad. Just steer clear of loud Pisceans, that's all.

BEING A LIBRA

Caring, sharing, and undecided about things — that's the Libran approach to life. If Libra is your Sun sign,

The typical Libra!

then your planet, Venus, will make sure that you have lots of friends, and that you are generally popular. It will also make you unsure as to which way to go in any decision, and unable to choose one person over another.

If you could lead your entire life without ever having an argument with anybody, then you would. Venus is the planet of all that's gentle and friendly; it puts all its energy into finding things to agree with and like rather than things to criticize and disapprove of. Venus' people, such as Librans (and Taureans too, whom you understand very well indeed) can always find something to like in everybody, and will think of that first rather than what you *don't* like.

It is really very simple: you find what you like, and then you spend time on it. If you don't like it, you don't do it. Now see how this simple principle gets misunderstood by your friends and family. If you have to do something which you don't like, you find other things to do instead, and you have no time to do your chore. When reminded, you say that you will get round to it soon, and genuinely mean to do so (you don't want an argument, do you? Librans hate disagreements), but somehow you find yourself drawn to something else. Some people say that this is lack of concentration, some people say it is laziness, but really it is neither. It is simply the strange influence of your planet, Venus, which automatically draws you towards the things which appeal to you, while those which don't appeal somehow slip away. Other star signs aren't like this. Some of them have a very strong sense of duty — Virgo, for example, the sign before you, which you dislike quite strongly at times — and some of them have a deep curiosity about things they don't like, testing them to see why it is that they don't like them: Scorpios are a bit like this. But not you.

Libra is the sign of the balance, and the idea of balance is one which is very important to you. You don't like it when there's too much of something in your life — too much work, too many bills to pay, even little things like too much of one colour when you're choosing your clothes, or too much furniture on one side of the room. Wherever there is imbalance, you feel compelled to do what you can to restore the correct proportions. It can lead to some odd results; although you do very well with the things which are yours to control, such as what you wear and what you say, your efforts to counterbalance a situation which is *not* under your control are sometimes harmful to you. You will, for example, put up with much abuse and unkindness from a partner when a relationship is deteriorating, and try to balance the situation by being extraordinarily considerate and generous in return. But then, a Libran will do almost anything rather than break a relationship, because the thing that Librans have to have, more than the other eleven signs, is a special companion or partner. Everybody likes having friends, but only the Libran cannot function properly without one. If you break up with your boyfriend, you will have a new one within a week. Some people think that this shows you as fickle, but it is nothing of the kind. It is simply that you cannot think straight unless you have a steady partner, somebody you can trust and feel close to. It's all to do with Venus again, forcing you to form attachments to the things you like. If you're not in a relationship, you're not being Libran; if you're not able to be yourself, as a Libran, you're not happy.

Most people have a special relationship; *one* special relationship, that is. Librans are different, because you form a special and almost intimate relationship with every single person you meet. The sign of Libra is the essence of relationship, or partnering, of being in twos; since you represent the energies of the sign in human form, you have to form one-to-one relationships with each person you meet. You're very, very good at it; there isn't anyone who doesn't find you attractive, and you can always find something about the other person that you like (Venus at work again) and make that the central theme of the partnership.

All this one-to-one pairing makes you much in demand socially, because you have the happy knack of making each person you talk to believe that he is somehow special, the only person in the world who matters to you. And you like flirting, too — you have to, because it's the only way that you communicate with people. I don't know whether you'd be so popular if your friends knew that your attractive friendliness was not for their particular benefit but because you simply can't behave any other way, but they don't know that, and I don't expect that you'll tell them.

Other people have physical energy, or mental energy, or intellectual energy; what Librans have is relationship energy. It's the only sort you've got, so you have to use it to do absolutely everything, and that takes people by surprise.

The only snag with all this is that you can *only* work on a one-to-one basis; when you're in a crowd of people you can't handle them all together, so you give your attention to several people separately, one after the other. If you've never noticed yourself doing that before, watch yourself next time you're out with a group of friends, and see.

Not that you could ever choose one person and abandon the others, of course: Librans, like all the zodiac's Air signs (the others are Gemini and Aquarius), need *variety*, like other people need food and love.

Librans are the biggest, most sentimental, total romantics ever made. The soft toy industry depends on you for its living, as do the publishers Mills and Boon. You probably have a small army of teddy bears, all with different names, all with different personalities, and you talk to them all in turn so that none of them feel neglected. You are forming relationships with things you like again, aren't you? Venus at work as usual. Another thing — Librans are very fair in their dealings; very fair indeed. This is why you go out with each of your friends in turn, and make sure each teddy gets a hug. You can also see both sides of any argument, and will of course be attracted to the good points of each. This means that you really can't decide which way to go, because it wouldn't be fair to the other side to pick one, would it?

Sentimental, fair-minded, indecisive, fond of your friends, and unable to bring yourself to tackle anything which you don't actually like — that's Libra, and it's all because of Venus. Still, you do have a monopoly on love and romance thanks to the same planet, so you can't grumble, can you?

BEING A SCORPIO

Intense, powerful, and passionate about things — that's the Scorpio approach to life. If Scorpio is your Sun sign, then Mars and Pluto, the planets which look after the sign, will give you the concentration and the strength to make anything that you want to happen, happen. It also makes you a fearsome enemy when control is taken from you and you feel that somebody else is trying to manipulate your life for you.

If, as a true Scorpio, you could live your life without ever having to compromise your Scorpionic principles, then you would have total power over everybody, know everything there was to know about everybody and their motives, be completely hidden from everybody unless you willed otherwise, and strike a mixture of fear and fascination into the hearts of those you chose to meet.

The key to this dark and passionate soul is the word *power*. Scorpios want it. Not the sort of show-off power of status symbols that your friends the Capricorns like,

The typical Scorpio!

though you understand that very well, nor the physical power that blazes out of the Aries; what a Scorpio wants is the real stuff, the invisible, string-pulling, controlling sort of power that makes people move when you use it. Whether you realize it or not, and whether they realize it or not (I'm sure they do, but they won't say), you are constantly trying to manipulate your friends, so that they do things your way. This isn't cruel or mean in any way, it's just the way you think. What you are trying to ensure is that you know how things are going to turn out, so that you won't be surprised. You don't like surprises much, because you might have to react to them in a way which would show the world what you are really like (if the world was watching, that is). You are very, very secretive about your true feelings, and wherever possible you try to keep them in check. You show feelings which are appropriate to the situation, sure; but your real feelings are a long way behind those, and only you know what they are. If you keep your feelings under control, you think to yourself, and you know how other people are going to behave, then you will always be in control of the situation. And that's how it works out, most of the time.

Of course, keeping everything under control means that you have to have considerable self-restraint, and also that you are going to be working at a much higher pressure than anyone else, and it's true, you do. What is visible on the outside of you is only a small fraction of the power that you have stored up inside you; whereas most people use most of their energy most of the time, you're always keeping yourself in check, holding back your full energies in case you need them in an emergency.

There are two main reasons why you do this. The first is because you won't let yourself get caught out without anything in reserve — if you were silly enough to give yourself one hundred per cent to something, you reckon, and it wasn't enough, then you'd be stuck, wouldn't you? All helpless and worn out, flapping about like a fish on the river bank. That's no way to be for a Scorpio. You'd have to rely on other people helping you then, and a Scorpio knows that he can *never* do that; it means being controlled by another person.

The second reason that you hold yourself back is that you're frightened of exploding. The amount of energy and passion inside you is truly enormous, and you fear that if you were really to let go, to give yourself over completely to blind rage, then there might not be a lot left of your world when the smoke cleared. You're right, Scorpio rage is a terrible thing, and it has to be controlled; on those occasions when Scorpios do let go, everybody gets hurt, including the Scorpio. Sometimes you feel compelled to do it, when you are trapped in a situation which is beyond your capabilities. In real life scorpions sting themselves to death, and zodiacal scorpions can do the same. It's like the self-destruct button which the mad scientist always has in the movies, and as a Scorpio you will know the fascination of it.

Staying in control of the situation means that you have to find out what's going on, and here's where another side of Scorpio gets developed. You have this great curiosity, a need to find things out, and winkle out secret facts from where they've been hidden. Scorpios make great detectives, and as for gossip and intrigue — you absolutely love it! There is no secret that you can't discover — but you're only discovering it for your own use, not so that it can become common knowledge. How stupid Geminis and Sagittarians seem to you: they tell everybody everything they know the minute they know it!

Hard work and turning your ambitions into realities are natural to you; once you have decided, then that's it — you get on with it, control the situation, and achieve it. That's how Mars works — energy in action. If things need changing to meet your requirements, then you rebuild them from their deepest foundations without a second thought. That's Pluto at work — the ability to start again from scratch if need be.

At the end of all this, you have considerable power, and there's nothing you like better than playing with it when you've got it. Scorpio ladies have a reputation as being *femmes fatales*; Mata Hari is the usual quoted example, but Princess Grace of Monaco was a Scorpio too, which makes you think a bit. Anyway, a Scorpio at play is a chance for you to ease the pressure, and to put some of your power store to some use. The opposite sex never resist the challenge and the concentrated passion of that Martian energy; they regard meeting a Scorpio as something of a dare, which they can't turn down. Your friends watch all this with amused fascination, and not a little jealousy — only you can get away with it, because only you are in control.

In a way, it's too easy for you to be attractive to the opposite sex, and from time to time it can get in the way of what you are trying to do. The reason for it is simply this: your own energies, Scorpio ones, are the energies of the planet Mars, astrologically speaking, which are the strongest and most direct of all. Other signs find it difficult to express themselves with this sort of passion and intensity, and generally reserve it for special occasions, or when the chemistry between two individuals makes it flow more easily. What they don't realize is that you do *everything* with the same sort of intensity, because you're built that way: you simply work at a higher voltage than the other signs. You do the most ordinary things, like clean your teeth, with the sort of concentrated force that they can only manage on special occasions. This means that when someone from another sign meets you, they interpret your actions as strong and passionate, and feel obliged to respond as best they can. This is all very well if you intend to form an intimate relationship with them, but rather inconvenient if you are merely being sociable. Most of the time, however, you don't mind; the effect you have on others amuses you, and usually means that they will do things your way, which is what you're after. Power, control, security, in that order.

BEING A SAGITTARIUS

A famous astrologer of the 1930s, asked which sign they'd like to be, given the choice, replied 'Sagittarius!'. The luckiest sign by far, its natives never worry, and never need to. You have flair, talent, imagination, and the ability to come out of the tightest scrapes sunny side up and smiling. How do you do it?

It's all because of the influence, through your sign, of the planet Jupiter. You Sagittarians are big people, even when you're small (which isn't often!). You are big-hearted, big-boned, and have big ideas. You are also big spenders and sometimes big-headed, but it doesn't seem to matter. This is because each and every one of you is full of the energy of the planet Jupiter, the biggest planet in the solar system. Jupiter gives us the word 'jovial': there is something about his influence that makes us smile, no matter what.

Jupiter is essentially good-natured, but he gets everywhere, and so does the Sagittarian. You have an insatiable curiosity about things, and would dearly love to know all there is to know about everything. To you, knowing things, and finding out more things to know, is fun. It never occurs to you that some things might be dangerous to know, dangerous to find out, or dangerous to tell people that you know; as far as you're concerned, knowledge is free for all to find and use, and you will tell anybody anything. Whatever your friends confide in you, you will tell to anyone else who asks; whatever occurs to you when you see somebody, you tell them straight, without ever thinking that they

The typical Sagittarius!

might not care to know. This openness and honesty (for that's all it is) gets you a reputation for tactlessness and gossiping which you feel is undeserved. In a way, it is; the inference is that you are in some way malicious, whereas the truth is that there is nobody in the zodiac more honest and fair than the Sagittarian. There is no reason for you to be dishonest, anyway; you don't even have to try to win if Jupiter is behind you.

Sagittarians are excited by the prospect of anything new, especially if it comes from far away. The romance of travel for its own sake is particularly yours; you can't think of anything worse than living in the same place for the rest of your life, and you can't think of anything better than a train ticket to Istanbul offered by a dark stranger. You know that the more things you see, the more things there will be to see, and you also know that you'll get through it all without serious mishap. Staying still, putting down roots and building a cosy family life sounds dreadful to an adventurer like you; new people and new experiences are what you long for.

There are two basic sorts of Sagittarians, and anybody who has ever attempted to tidy your bedroom will be able to tell you which one you are, if you don't already know. First are the intellectual sorts, who read books on anything and everything. Novels, travel, history, anything at all. If you are one of these, you can never pass a bookshop without going in and buying at least three, often on subjects that you had never thought of until you saw the book in the shop. You are probably good at languages; you are the sort who can learn a language from the waiters on holiday.

The second sort of Sagittarian is the sporty and active sort. If it involves movement, you do it. Riding, skiing, and all motorized sports appeal, because they get you there faster, and that's what you really enjoy, isn't it? You probably have a vast collection of bags; the reason is that you keep thinking that you will need them to put things in when you next travel somewhere, which would ideally be at a moment's notice. Depressed Sagittarians are usually to be found buying bags or maps, or thumbing through travel brochures — the very idea of going somewhere cheers you up.

Despite Jupiter's influence and help, you do have one or two faults, but somehow everyone tends not to notice them. One of the biggest is your inability to see anything on a small scale; you're full of grand ideas and wonderful schemes, but the little details that make them work are too small for you to grasp, and you make mistakes. Spending time with fiddly things annoys you — you're impatient to be finished and on to the next thing, and as you wrestle with a jammed lock on a suitcase, or a faulty telephone, your patience evaporates almost at once. Rather than take your time, you're more likely to leave it behind or do without it altogether.

The same thing happens at work, too. You can see the principles and the eventual aim of the job at once, but the details which have to be learned so that it is performed properly don't interest you, and although you ought to be able to master them with your eyes closed, almost, you make silly slips because you have become bored. Your carelessness doesn't count against you, though, because most people don't mind the odd error here and there — in fact they prefer you like that to someone who gets everything right and is always perfect. Virgos, who are good at detail but very poor at seeing the larger view, are much less popular than Sagittarians, so it appears that even your faults work to your advantage. There's Sagittarianism for you.

The greatest quality that you have is optimism. It never really crosses your mind that things won't turn out well in the end; 'happily ever after' is a statement of fact to you, whereas the other eleven signs know that only fairy tales end like that. Whenever you are down, or when outside pressures are making life a bit of a squeeze, you can always find something to catch your attention and lift your spirits, and more often than not use it to provide a solution to your difficulties. This requires more than mere chance, it requires a lifelong, never-failing streak of pure luck, and Sagittarians have exactly that in the form of Jupiter, which never lets you down. Knowing that you will always manage, somehow, means that you get to be more careless with yourself and your efforts than you might be, whereas other signs work hard and save their earnings for rainy days.

That same optimism applies to your personal relationships, too. When you're in love, you give your partner everything you've got, like a big, boisterous puppy, and it's sometimes a bit much for the other person to take. It's not that they don't like you, but your enthusiasm is rather overwhelming, especially in the first stages of a relationship.

Sagittarians aren't the most constant lovers. Anything new is interesting to you for that very reason, and so a new person is always more interesting than someone you already know, no matter how close you are. Sagittarian optimism always says that the next person will be even better — and even when that proves not to be true, you know that the *next* one will be, and so on. It also never occurs to you that the ones you leave behind you are at all upset; you didn't mean to hurt them, after all, and you don't feel upset yourself, so why should they?

As you can see, you can be a bit naive about emotions at times. This is because you don't need anyone else as an emotional support, thanks to Jupiter. Nor do you want anyone to be dependent on you; you like the freedom to chase after new ideas, new people and new places. What you're really after is someone who likes your company as much as you like theirs, and who is with you because they think it's fun. People like this are hard to find, but you'll keep looking — and with your luck, you'll probably find them.

BEING A CAPRICORN

Hardworking, rather serious, but successful at whatever you attempt — that's the Capricorn right through. If Capricorn is your Sun-sign, then Saturn, the planet that looks after both the sign and you in it, will make sure that you get to your rightful place at the top of the pile — but only in return for a lot of work.

You're a pretty cool character, for the most part. You Capricorns, and your neighbours the Aquarians, are notably cool. You are cool emotionally, in that you don't get excited and flustered when things start to happen a bit faster than expected, and you are cool in relationships too. Don't think that you don't have feelings — you do; but they are not on the surface, and not expressed, which is what makes you different from the rest of us. You know what you want, and you know how to get it; you also know that getting in a spin won't help, so you don't let yourself get that way.

It is all Saturn's doing. He moves very slowly around the sky, and he gives the Capricorn a state of mind that works in very long periods of time. Some people can only think as far as the next meal; some can plan forward until tomorrow or the next week. Some people even look forward to next year's holidays. You, Capricorn, are thinking about where you will be five or ten *years*' time. And where will you be in ten years' time? On top, on the board, in the chairman's seat. To you, everything is structured. There are people in charge, and people above them, and directors above them, and so on. Right at the top, you figure, is where you'd like to be. Where you ought to be. Where you're going to be. When you're there, everyone will know it, and give you the respect you deserve. Power, position, reputation; these are what the Capricorn wants. You are capable of handling the responsibility, and you are capable of doing the work involved, so there is no problem; it is simply a matter of time and effort, and

The typical Capricorn!

Capricorns are blessed not only with the ability to see forward in ten or twenty year stages, but also with an unequalled capacity for work.

Saturn also gives you endurance, the ability to keep going for a long time, for as long as it takes. Other signs are quick and firm in their actions where you are not, but long after they have given up the struggle you will still be pushing onwards. Some signs are like sprinters, and some are like shot putters; Capricorns are marathon runners. If achieving your ambitions takes years, then so be it; but you'll get there in the end, and you will win, too.

Your way of seeing things as being part of a structure, with everything in its place, extends into Time, as well. If this sounds difficult to comprehend, then think of the idea of *tradition*. Tradition is to do with previous generations doing things for those still to come, and to do with those of the present day carrying on the work that their predecessors began, so that their successors will have something to inherit. The idea of doing things in the way that they have always been done is one which makes a great deal of sense to the Capricornian mind. You don't do things in the old-fashioned way because you are short of imagination and initiative, as some of the other signs — notably Sagittarians — might unfairly suggest, but because to you the old way is the best way. If generations of people have learned by experience that one way is better, then you are pleased to make use of their experience. You don't feel that you have to make your mark in society for being different; you feel, instead, that you have good work to carry on, and that what you have inherited is also your responsibility, and that you must hand it on in as good, if not better, condition as when it came to you. To transform anything unnecessarily, or to lessen it in any way, would be to fail in your responsibility.

To work in the way that you do means that you must

have a very strong belief in the order of things, and in
the rightness of that order. That belief is there in every
Capricorn, strong enough not only to govern your own
actions, but enough to make you impose your views on
those around you and beneath you, as well. And a good
job, too: if Capricorns weren't there to provide a
framework for the rest of us, society would fall apart.
Each sign has a job to perform for the others, and yours
is to hold us all together.

It sounds as though Capricorns suffer from too much
work and not enough play, but in fact you are a great
person to socialize with. It is true that you take things
very seriously, and have little in the way of light chat,
but you are so forceful and ambitious, such a
determined achiever, that you have a special energy all
your own, and it gives you a special glamour. You also
have a chance to display your sense of humour when
you're amongst friends. Your idea of humour is very
sharp, and very dry. Sarcastic one-liners are very
much your style, and much appreciated by those who
know you well. Your humour can be wounding, though,
to those meeting it for the first time.

Capricorns play as hard as they work, and you play
with the things that your hard work has brought you;
you love expensive toys, so that you can show
everybody what you've achieved. Designer clothes
with visible names are a Capricorn thing, as are pieces
of status jewellery like watches, rings, and lighters. You
take a great deal of pride in your car, too, which to you
is something with which you can show your rank and
position.

Your sense of tradition and duty comes into your
personal life, too. Capricorns aren't really much given
to short-term relationships, because it seems such a
waste to spend several months of time, effort, and
money on something which won't last. What you're
after is a relationship which can be built on, something
which will get stronger as it gets older, and which can

become part of the structure of your career and family. What you're prepared to give is time and effort, the same things that you give to anything else, and what you want in return is commitment and reliability. Anyone who becomes your partner is going to have a successful and comfortable lifestyle — you will make sure of that — but if they want either a light romance or overwhelming passion then they have picked the wrong person, because you never let your emotional expression take precedence over your responsibilities. Capricorns have something of a reputation as forceful lovers, actually; it is said that all the zodiac signs with horns — Aries, Taurus, Capricorn — are talented in this respect. That may be so, but you keep such diversions until later, when you have some time to yourself, and when you have finished doing what you have to, what you ought to, and what is expected of you.

Ambitious, determined, hardworking — that's the essence of Capricorn, and it's all due to Saturn. He makes you a winner in the long term, and keeps you on course, but he prevents you from taking pleasure from things which occur on the spur of the moment. A small price to pay for the thing that you have over the rest of us, which is that as you get older, you get better. The other eleven signs can't do that.

BEING AN AQUARIAN

Cool, aloof, and independent — that's the Aquarian approach to life. Unlike most of the zodiac signs, Aquarius has two planets instead of one to look after it: Saturn to keep you cool and collected, and Uranus to make you just that little bit special, a bit different from everybody else.

Aquarians are the friendliest people in the whole zodiac. The ideal life for you, as an Aquarian, is one where you have a lot of company, arranged in different

The typical Aquarius!

circles; one group of friends from work, one group of old school friends, a bunch of people from the tennis club, and so on. It doesn't seem a good idea to you to be too closely involved with one group of people.

It seems even less of a good idea to be too closely tied to one person; that would mean that you sacrificed your independence. Independence is the essential thing for an Aquarian; you don't need to feel that you belong with anybody, or that somebody needs you in a special way. You are quite happy being yourself, thanks. The person who needs you most is *you*.

It's not that you are cold and heartless — far from it. You are actually very kind and considerate, and will often give a lot of your time and effort to what strikes you as a deserving case at the time. Afterwards, when everybody wants to thank you, you are surprised and dismissive: 'Oh, that. Oh, that's okay, it was no trouble.' Notice how cool you sound; that's very Aquarian. You get involved when you want to, and you let your involvement drop when you want to, you're the one who says when, and that's how you like it — independent.

That coolness carries on into your personal life, too. The relationships you enjoy most are the ones where you have a really good friendship with someone rather than an obsession. It's not that you're not passionate, or that you can't express yourself physically, it's simply that the meeting of minds matters more to you than the meeting of bodies. A sparkling dual of wit and logic between two people with clear ideas and strong wills is what really excites you. At all times, you like to feel that you are clear in your own mind about what you are thinking and what your opinion is: if you become emotionally dependent on somebody, or obsessed with them, then your clear thinking becomes woolly, and you don't like that.

Some signs look forward to being in love, so that they can lose themselves in the rush of passion which alters their view of reality, but to an Aquarian that sounds like the worst thing imaginable. You always want to be fully alert, mentally, so that you keep your own identity. A bright and stimulating friendship, with shared interests and ambitions, will allow you to keep your own identity, while enjoying the company of someone who is similar, but different. That's the ideal state of affairs for you.

Although you stay cool about individual relationships, you do get pretty heated about big issues. Many Aquarians are active campaigners for political or ecological movements, and their views can seem a little extreme to the rest of us. Are you for the complete prohibition of all motor vehicles, or the abolition of Parliament? Whatever your views, they will be for the best of reasons, because Aquarians have a genuine concern for everyone's welfare. Any system which is to the advantage of one person at the expense of many others is a bad thing, in an Aquarian's view. You are passionately opposed to *all* forms of hierarchy, and strongly believe that everyone is basically the same as everyone else, and should be treated accordingly. This very democratic viewpoint is exactly the opposite of the view held by the sign before you, Capricorn, and that's one reason why you find them so difficult to get on with.

You are quite prepared to fight for your views, and to oppose any system which you feel is unfair. This draws quite a few of you into politics, usually at a local level; that's where the inequalities are most obvious, and where you feel that the changes have to be made. You will make sure everyone knows that your actions are for the benefit of everyone, and not just for yourself; putting yourself in a higher position is against Aquarian principles. Aquarian principles are very high, and very pure; you think with a very brutal sort of logic which leaves any emotional considerations out of the argument altogether — and when you have come to an opinion, you will stick to it, because you know that it is logically correct. Mr Spock, from *Star Trek*, must be an Aquarian: he certainly thinks like one.

Not that you are serious all the time, of course; most of the time you keep your opinions to yourself until asked, and let other people have their say instead. You love to hear what everyone else has got to say for themselves; Aquarius is an Air sign, like Libra and Gemini, and to all of you ideas and conversation are as important as food and water. Without variety and lively company you can become depressed, or even ill, so wherever there is conversation and argument, there you are. Not that you are likely to accept anyone else's point of view once you've heard it, though: it is an essential part of Aquarianism to be separate and independent from anybody else, not the same in any way. Besides, your faultless logic has already provided you with what you consider to be the right answer.

Luckily for all your friends, you are not tempted to correct their wrong opinions in the way that a Sagittarian is, and from time to time you will even suggest something controversial just for the fun of it when you think that a conversation is getting dull. You love the surprise on everybody's face when you say it; it reminds both you and them that you are independent and different, and you like that.

You are great fun to be with. Anybody with a sense of adventure, and who likes looking at things from an unusual viewpoint, will find your self-assured, but friendly, nature very attractive. Sagittarians and Arians are bright and active, and neither of them are much interested in making deep and lasting commitments, so they make good friends for you. They appreciate your modern outlook, too. Aquarian thought always looks to what comes next rather than what went before, and that means an interest in new technology and new inventions — but not much sense of history. That's another reason why you don't get on with Capricorns.

Your modern outlook, your fight to change things

which are wrong even if they have been accepted for years, and your love of conversation and argument are all part of the way that you show your independence, and it is this quality which more than anything else is the key to the Aquarian personality. Whatever else you do you must always feel that you are not like anyone else, you are unique.

There are a number of little tricks that you use to keep your independence. One of them is being on your own: when you are on your own you can think about things coolly, and perhaps laugh at yourself a little for getting so involved with someone or something. When you need a little time on your own, you can usually arrange it, somehow. Being in a different room, or going on a little errand to get you out of the office for five minutes, or simply being out doing something else to avoid being in when someone calls — you do all of these. You are not hiding, you are simply putting yourself at a distance to maintain your independence. That's Aquarius.

BEING A PISCES

Sensitive, imaginative, intuitive — but indecisive, changeable, and unrealistic, too. Pisces is all of these, and more. There are two planets specifically associated with the sign, Jupiter and Neptune, but neither of them lend their energies to practical things; both of them are to do with expanding the imagination, and letting your feelings run free. No wonder the other signs seem dull and dutiful by comparison!

You are the chameleons of the zodiac; you're not sure what you like or dislike, but when you are near something which seems interesting or exciting to you, then you will take on its appearance and behaviour so that you resemble it. A Piscean girl who is trying to impress a new boyfriend who is keen on car racing

The typical Pisces!

suddenly finds herself interested in cars; if your partner happens to be keen on opera you find yourself dressing up for first nights. It's not that you don't enjoy any of these things; you enjoy them immensely once you get into them, but in every case what you are doing is absorbing the initial enthusiasm from somebody else, and making it part of yourself.

Why do you behave like this? Is it normal? Well, no, in that none of the other eleven signs do it, but all Pisceans do it, because a Piscean is active by being reactive; in other words, you only do anything in response to something which has had an effect on you; you never make the first move yourself.

Pisceans are sensitive to absolutely anything — the slightest hint of emotion in a snatch of conversation, the colour of your surroundings, the feel of your clothes. The other eleven signs have no idea how strongly you are affected by things which they simply wouldn't notice. Next time somebody tells you that they don't understand you, tell them that you are like the film in a camera; you are sensitive to, and will faithfully represent, anything you are exposed to, even if it is only light and shadow, and only for a second.

To be as sensitive as this obviously makes you emotionally vulnerable. The other two water signs, Cancer and Scorpio, have developed hard outer shells so that they hide their feelings, just like the animals of their signs; but what do Piscean fish do? Swim away, of course. Your defence against things which make you uncomfortable is simply to run away, to escape. You have a bit of a reputation for avoiding responsibility and for slipping away when a situation gets tight, but all you are doing is escaping the pressure. To someone as sensitive as yourself, emotional pressure of any kind is actually painful; what is more natural than to move to where the pressure is eased? Fish have various mechanisms to ease the pressure of the water on them, and Pisceans, who are human fish swimming in a sea of emotions and impressions, have similar mechanisms. All very easy when it's explained, isn't it?

The other thing that Pisceans can do is to become invisible. This is what you do when you can't run away, but you still want to ease the pressure. I don't know how you do it, but you seem to have the ability to become part of the wallpaper, unseen by everyone else, and safe from being spotted. When you hope that you won't be noticed or asked what you think, you just seem to make yourself transparent, somehow, and the focus of attention goes somewhere else, leaving you untouched. It's a neat trick, and unique to your sign.

Your two biggest talents are imagination and sympathy. The imagination shows itself in just about any field of artistic activity; you have a way with words and images, and the associations that they bring to mind, which is the best in the zodiac. It's not surprising, really, when you think that your mind works almost entirely on an emotional level rather than a practical one, but it means that Pisceans are very much in demand at the moment. The industries which depend on presenting attractive images — film, television, video, magazines, advertising — all need Pisceans to come up with the right idea, the right picture, the right *feel* for what they want to say. A hundred years ago, all that some astrology books had to say about Pisceans was that they were 'addicted to drink and gambling', but in the twentieth century your imagination has been your fortune.

That other Piscean emotion, sympathy, is every bit as strong as your talented imagination. When someone is suffering or in pain, you can feel it as strongly as heat or cold, because you are so sensitive to such things. Your response is immediate sympathy, and by providing that you help ease the other person's discomfort, and so feel less of it yourself. Their pain hurts you, when you are near it, so you work to reduce it.

The only other zodiac sign which has an emotional

response like yours is Cancer — but Cancer gives protection and support whereas you give sympathy! They are similar, but not the same.

Movement is very important to a Piscean. If you can't feel yourself moving along through life, you wonder why. What you like best is the feeling you get when you can combine movement and emotion, somehow expressing the one through the other; this is why so many Pisceans are interested in the Arts, the theatre, and most of all in dance and ballet. It's not because Pisceans are graceful — often you're not — but because you instinctively understand the link between feelings and movement. This is why you don't like being in a situation which closes you in or expects you to play a definite role; it would restrict the number of new things for you to react to, it would prevent you from escaping. If you're not free to move and change, you don't like it.

There are times when you really are trapped, though. As you will know very well, in those situations you escape into your imagination, through music or a book. The great thing about a Piscean, which none of the down-to-earth or practical signs ever understand, is that things are only real to you if you believe them to be so — when reality is painful, you can replace it with an imaginative fantasy and believe in that until things get better. Only Pisces has this *internal* escape route. Have a good look at yourself; are you using it more than you should? A lot of Pisceans do, because it's so much easier for you to think of nicer things, but on some occasions you have to do what's necessary for yourself. Think of the Piscean fish again: salmon swim upstream each year, returning to the rivers where they were born. It isn't easy for them to swim against the current, but they do it all the same. Pisceans can swim upstream too, when they have to.

2
QUIZ: HOW TYPICAL ARE YOU?

Here's a simple way to find out how close to being the textbook sign you are. There are two sets of questions, Section A and Section B. Just choose the answer which seems closest to the way you feel or would act in that situation, and check your score at the end.

SECTION A

1. If you met an intruder in your garden one night, would you
   (a)   have a go at him?
   (b)   tell him it was your garden and would he please leave?
   (c)   try to reason with him?
   (d)   run away or hide?

2. When you go to the movies, do you choose
   (a)   an all-action picture with a dynamic hero?
   (b)   something glamorous and easy on the eye?
   (c)   a film with a message, maybe a foreign language film?
   (d)   a love story or a weepie?

3. What appeals to you most in a person of the opposite sex?
   (a)   Their body.

(b) Their lifestyle.
(c) Their lively conversation.
(d) Their kindness and concern.

4. What do you want out of a job?
(a) Excitement and challenge.
(b) Power, responsibility, and money.
(c) Variety and interesting people.
(d) Security

5. When talking to somebody new, are you
(a) honest and open, saying anything you feel like?
(b) keen that they should form a good impression of you?
(c) happy to embroider the truth a little as you go along, to keep the conversation sparkling?
(d) shy and reserved, letting slip very little about yourself?

6. What do you like to do with your money?
(a) Spend it on outrageous and amusing things for yourself.
(b) Spend it on quality possessions which will last.
(c) Spend it on your friends, on socializing, and on holidays.
(d) Save it, in case you need it for anything.

7. How do you see children?
(a) Good, boisterous fun.
(b) The future of your family, a responsibility but a bit noisy.
(c) Lively, talkative, amusing companions.
(d) Endearing souls who need your love and care.

8. How would you describe your style of dress?
(a) Dynamic.
(b) Classic.

(c) Informal.
(d) Romantic/Seductive.

9. Which of these would you most like to live in?
(a) A villa in Italy or the South of France.
(b) An eight-bedroomed mansion with a gravel drive, tennis courts and a swimming pool.
(c) A Manhattan penthouse with a fabulous view of New York.
(d) A lovely little cottage by the waterside.

10. If your fairy godmother gave you a wish, would you choose
(a) lifelong fame?
(b) lifelong wealth?
(c) to be clever, witty, and popular?
(d) to have true love for ever?

SECTION B

1. If you inherited a country house in some disrepair, would you
(a) make plans to fix it and extend it with new additions of your own?
(b) restore it to its former glory and maintain it in that condition?
(c) convert it into something else, like an hotel or a conference centre?

2. It's your first day in a new job. Do you
(a) do it the way you think best?
(b) find out how your predecessor did things, and copy his way of working?
(c) ask around, establish communication, see what was wrong before, and what you can bring to the problem now?

3. Would you rather
  (a)   make things?
  (b)   buy things?
  (c)   sell things?

4. On arrival at your holiday destination you find that your hotel room is double-booked. Do you
  (a)   Complain, arrange a full refund on the spot, and march off to see if any of the other hotels in town have anything suitable?
  (b)   Stay where you are and refuse to move until you get your room?
  (c)   Try to come to an arrangement with the management, taking a smaller room and some financial compensation as well?

5. Which of these do you find the most attractive quality in a person?
  (a)   Initiative.
  (b)   Reliability.
  (c)   Tolerance.

6. What kind of career are you aiming for?
  (a)   Something where you can get to the top.
  (b)   Something stable and secure, where you can make steady progress until you get your pension.
  (c)   Nothing, really just a series of different jobs which you take as the interest and opportunity arise.

7. Is your dream car
  (a)   A pure performance car, not necessarily reliable or practical?
  (b)   A head-turning limousine with every possible refinement?
  (c)   A truly versatile all-rounder, able to do everything well and to go anywhere with ease?

8. In making decisions, do you
   (a) make instant judgements and stick to them?
   (b) try not to be too hasty, and take the safe option?
   (c) change your mind once or twice before reaching a final conclusion?

9. Some project you have worked on for a long time breaks down and collapses completely. Do you
   (a) shrug your shoulders, then make a start on something different, without a backward glance?
   (b) do whatever is necessary to repair it and rebuild it bit by bit, since total loss is unthinkable?
   (c) see if any parts of it are worth salvaging and using in something else?

10. Think of your least attractive physical feature. Would you like it to be
   (a) better?
   (b) bigger?
   (c) different?

How Did You Score?

If you chose mostly (a)s in Section A and mostly (a)s in Section B, then your responses are typical of an Aries.

If you chose mostly (a)s in Section A and mostly (b)s in Section B, then your responses are typical of a Leo.

If you chose mostly (a)s in Section A and mostly (c)s in Section B, then your responses are typical of a Sagittarius.

If you chose mostly (b)s in Section A and mostly (a)s in Section B, then your responses are typical of a Capricorn.

If you chose mostly (b)s in Section A and mostly (b)s in Section B, then your responses are typical of a Taurus.

If you chose mostly (b)s in Section A and mostly (c)s in Section B, then your responses are typical of a Virgo.

If you chose mostly (c)s in Section A and mostly (a)s in Section B, then your responses are typical of a Libra.

If you chose mostly (c)s in Section A and mostly (b)s in Section B, then your responses are typical of an Aquarius.

If you chose mostly (c)s in Section A and mostly (c)s in Section B, then your responses are typical of a Gemini.

If you chose mostly (d)s in Section A and mostly (a)s in Section B, then your responses are typical of a Cancer.

If you chose mostly (d)s in Section A and mostly (b)s in Section B, then your responses are typical of a Scorpio.

If you chose mostly (d)s in Section A and mostly (c)s in Section B, then your responses are typical of a Pisces.

Don't worry if you find that your responses belong to a different sign from your Sun sign. It doesn't mean that you have answered incorrectly, or that astrology is rubbish, or somebody has been telling you lies about when your birthday is. What it means is that your birth sign is outweighed by other factors in your horoscope, such as the position of the Moon, or the rising sign (see page 216), which are probably in other signs. This will make you think and react in the manner of the other signs, rather than the one you were born under — it's part of what makes everybody unique.

3
LIFESTYLES

ARIES

Home

Arians don't spend a great deal of time at home, and so it tends to function as a base depot rather than a retreat from the world or an expression of your wealth and taste. Arian taste is strong, and not very subtle, so if there's anything you particularly like, your house will have a lot of it. What you like are strong colours, and large solid pieces of furniture: pastel tones and delicate draperies aren't your style at all. You like anything strong and vivid, so the pictures you have on the walls won't be restful landscapes or gentle watercolours. There's plenty of stuff around, the place isn't at all bare, but nothing is there because it's pretty, or ornamental, or has sentimental value; Arians look forward, not back, and the idea of anything being pretty for its own sake escapes you completely. Generally, frilliness and over-femininity is something you avoid, and you don't like it when you meet it in someone else's home.

What you do like, for yourself, are new toys. Arians are all kids at heart, and any little mechanical gadget, especially one which you've never seen before, delights you. Your house has lots of them, and you're always pleased to get another one as a present.

Cars

The Arian view of a car is as one of life's finer things. One of the qualities which you enjoy about yourself is the capacity you have for moving quickly when the need arises, and you get a real kick out of your own performance being that bit quicker than everyone else's. With a car, you can move faster still, and the pleasure of driving at speed is something that never loses its appeal for you.

Driving a car is something very close to your heart: every part of the process appeals enormously to your Arian nature. You can feel a car's power pull you along as though it had your own muscles, and the sound of its exhaust is music to your ears, not 'noise'. It may surprise you to know that other signs are not like this, and your own enjoyment of speed and machinery for their own sake is one which you share only with Scorpio and Sagittarius, and even then their enthusiasm isn't quite the same as yours. Other signs like their cars to be quiet, so that they can't hear anything of the engine, and they like the car to float along serenely, so that there is no sensation of speed or travelling. You may find some signs who don't care for performance, either, and aren't interested in travelling quickly. Unimaginable to an Aries, but perfectly reasonable to them. Finally, there are some signs who don't want their cars to draw attention to themselves — they see a car as a suit of armour which protects them from the outside world, and lets them go here and there in the safety of their own little shell.

Not you. What you want is a car which will advertise you to the world, expressing that Arian energy in an unmistakable way, so that everyone who sees you going by will be impressed by its power and strength, and will know that its owner is an Arian.

You want your car to be fast, and you want it to be a driver's car — to *feel* fast as well as *be* fast, and to *feel* in contact with the road, exactly matching your movements at the wheel with its own. You also want it to sound good: rushing wind, squealing tyres, and roaring exhaust are all part of the fun of driving for you, and you want them there to add to your excitement. And colour? You'd like it to be red, if possible; none of your discreet metallic greys or neutral cream colours — you want your car scarlet. It doesn't matter to you if it only has room for two people, or if it has no room for luggage, or if it's expensive to run. What matters is that it must perform: anything else can be ignored.

In an ideal world, you'd have a Ferrari. In the real world, you'll settle for a sporty coupé (provided they're red, of course). You're in two minds about most of the high-performance hatchbacks, though; they're all a bit short and stubby in outline, and an Arian likes his cars to look long and low. Ten years ago Arians all bought high-powered Fords, because the shape and the performance were just right, but the sportsters of the late 1980s are generally too quiet and too civilized to have true Arian appeal. One thing, though, you'd *never* buy is an estate car or a pick-up.

Food

Although you may enjoy eating, food isn't usually one of the major interests in your life. With the Earth signs, such as Taurus, food is almost the centre of existence, but Aries is a Fire sign, with Leo and Sagittarius, and what Fire signs need food for is to give them the energy to carry on with whatever else they're doing.

You do have definite preferences, all the same. Fire signs like their food to have a bit of chewing in it, to have some real texture, and they like strong flavours, too. Bland food, which tastes of nothing in particular, and which is soft and without substance, doesn't appeal to you at all.

What you really like is meat. All Fire signs are supposed to be great meat-eaters, and Aries is said to be the biggest meat-eater of the three. All that protein gives you something to get your teeth into, and it also gives you the energy to keep going at the rate you do. And it's red, too, which you find attractive. A plate with a great red piece of meat on it looks like a meal to an Arian, whereas a plate of vegetables is altogether too green. It sounds funny, but you know what you like when you see it, and to look attractive to you a plate mustn't have too much green; an Arian doesn't like it.

It really is the colour of food that influences you rather than the vegetables themselves, because you're quite fond of red vegetables, such as tomatoes or red peppers, and when you have a choice, such as at a buffet where you serve yourself, you will find yourself choosing dishes with tomatoes in rather than the green salad.

Red peppers are a favourite for more than their colour; they are also hot, of course, and Arians love all hot or spicy flavours. Chillies and curries are a special favourite, and you like peppered steak, too. It's all to do with the Fire sign, you see.

The Arian liking for the colour red and for spices continues into the dessert course too, and your favourites include things like apple pie with cinnamon, or anything with cherries in it. Cherry cheesecake, with an attractive red topping, is always enticing to an Arian. You even prefer pink yogurt, like cherry or raspberry flavour, against the other flavours and colours.

Finally, of course, you like red wine. Better still, in winter, is mulled wine, surely the ultimate Arian drink: it's red, it's hot, and it's spicy — what more could you want?

Holidays

All Fire signs like travelling; to go somewhere new has the promise of new adventures, and you like that. Lots of Arians take their cars abroad on holiday and drive to wherever they're going, because they love their cars so much, but wherever you go, and whether you drive or fly, you'd like to be heading for somewhere that has a bit of a reputation to it, somewhere exciting. The last thing you need on holiday is a quiet time, dozing away a fortnight in a little village where nothing ever happens. It will drive you insane. What an Arian needs is something to do, something which will give you a buzz, and something which will keep your high energy level fully occupied.

The actual location isn't so important to you. You don't have a particular need to be by the sea, or to see beautiful scenery; what matters to you is what you're actually doing during your holiday, and if you have plenty to do and you think it's fun, then you'll be more than satisfied. Your only preference, as far as your surroundings go, is for heat: Fire signs like warm climates, so you choose accordingly.

Some sort of sporting holiday, where you're kept busy doing something athletic and fairly strenuous, would be just perfect for you. Even if there isn't anything like that available where you are, you'll soon find a few other like-minded souls to make up a game of beach volleyball, or something to keep you busy. And if there is any possibility of hiring a car in your holiday resort, you'll be first in the queue. Arians just won't sit still!

Not many people positively enjoy danger and risk, but Arians do, and if the place you go for a holiday has a rather dangerous air to it then you'll like it all the more. Two places in Europe which are specifically connected with Aries are Marseilles and Naples, and both of them have the sort of reputation you'll find attractive.

There are plenty of quieter, and prettier places which are Arian, though, and which you might like to try. England itself is an Arian country, and so is Germany, but to go further south in search of the sun you might like to try Burgundy, in the heart of France. In Italy, the beautiful Arian cities of Florence and Padua await you, but if you're really in search of the sun, then Israel, which also has Aries as its zodiac sign, is probably your best bet.

Drinks

Arians are very direct about drinking and bars. Some signs use their local for socializing, and some as a sort of market-place where they buy and sell things, but Arians simply go for a drink, and they drink because they're thirsty. It's as simple as that.

The same simplicity can be seen in the way you go in, as well. You go through the door, up to the bar, and ask for a drink. It is possible to draw a straight line, most of the time, between the door and where you're standing. People from other zodiac signs, you will be amazed to learn, do things like making sure that they're not in line with the door, making for the darkest corner, sitting near the back, and all sort of funny things — but Arians do things in the most simple and straightforward way, as always.

The same applies to what you drink, too. Male Arians drink beer, because it's easily available and because it quenches thirst. The idea of drinking something because it is fashionable or because it has been heavily advertised to give it some status is lost on you, to a large extent. Female Arians have similarly simple tastes, but when you're feeling like something a little more exotic you enjoy a Bloody Mary — vodka and tomato juice — because of its colour, that unmistakable Arian red.

You're not the sort of person who will only drink in one place. Some signs prefer one pub, their local, to any other, and mutter gloomily if forced to go somewhere else at the request of the people they're with, but you don't mind. Besides, the sort of active life you lead means that you are often in many different places, and when you get thirsty you go to wherever's nearest. As long as you can get a drink when you need one, you're not fussy.

Sports and pastimes

Arians are the world's most natural athletes. You don't need to learn to use your body — you were born doing it, and you will continue to do so for the rest of your life. It's the way you function. As a result, you can become very good indeed at almost anything athletic that you have a go at, *and* in a much shorter time than it takes for the other signs. You are at your best in those sports where you are the only player, such as running, jumping or throwing things — track and field athletics, mainly. You are less good in team games, because you are impatient to get your turn, or to have the ball passed to you, or whatever, and although you're quite good at racquet sports, you're more interested in your own performance — and in winning — than in the game itself. What you really like to do is to push yourself to perform better than you did last time, and you don't necessarily need another player for that.

Aries is good at combat sports, too, such as the martial arts, or boxing. The advantage of the sign is a talent for striking, for punching and hitting things in explosive bursts, and that makes you a better boxer than wrestler, better at karate than judo. You might be better still at kendo, or at sabre fencing; Aries works very well with metal instruments, but they need to be quite large and heavy to bring out the best in you; the lighter techniques of fencing with a foil are best suited to other signs.

Aries likes mechanized sports, too — it's the affinity with metal again — so all forms of motor sport, on two wheels and on four, appeal to you, and so does shooting.

Away from the playing fields, and out of the garage, you're still happier with a metal implement in your hand than without. You're more than happy to work around the house or in the garden, but you like digging or building best, because those are the sort of jobs that you can really make your muscles work at, and that's what you like best.

You like music, but you like it loud, and with a strong beat to it, and you will probably enjoy the process of building up a sound system of sufficient power and complexity to give you the volume you enjoy. Playing music for yourself isn't really an Arian thing, but those Arians who do find that brass instruments (metal again) have more appeal than stringed ones.

Colour and style

It is often said that Arians have no time for fashion, because they are too busy dashing around. That's very true, and it gives an important clue to the Arian style, which is that movement is everything.

You need to be able to move, and to move easily. From time to time fashion may dictate that tight or constricting clothes are the style of the moment, but on you they look as though somebody has tried to tie you up, because you will always be moving faster than the clothes will let you, and the strain on both you and the outfit will be visible. Clothes which look best when the wearer is sitting down and being elegantly inactive just won't work, because you're quite simply never still for long enough. What you need is something which lets you move, though that needn't mean huge and shapeless.

A lot of Arians dress in sports wear, such as tracksuits and training shoes, more than they need to. They look good on you, because of your athletic build, but almost anything looks good on an Arian for this very reason. Arians are strong, direct people, and should dress to show this. Strong lines in the cut, and bold areas of solid colour show Arian energy well. What you should avoid is anything with a small or fussy pattern, because the match between the small design and the big Arian personality really doesn't work.

The best way for you to show the world how you feel, and to feel good at the same time, is to dress in your zodiacal colour. You'll know what your colour is by now — it's the colour of your favourite car, your favourite food, your favourite anything. Bright red. Everybody else looks outrageous in pure red, but Arians just look Arian. It's yours, so wear it as often as you like.

Work

Arians need their jobs to contain three things: activity, movement, and initiative. If the job itself doesn't keep you busy from morning till night, you get bored, and start looking around for something else to do. If the job doesn't make any real progress but is always the same, day after day, then you feel disheartened, because you need to feel that you are achieving something and can look back to see how far you've come. Similarly, if the job keeps you behind a desk all day, and you never see anything but the same four walls, then you feel that you're not making the best use of yourself. Finally, if the job doesn't present fresh challenges, inspiring you to find solutions of your own devising to problems which have never arisen before, then you feel that there's nothing for you to get your teeth into, and you become frustrated and dissatisfied.

All this makes an Arian very easy to employ, and very hard to retain; your willingness to start on anything new — and the energy you put into mastering it — means that you can make a good start in almost any job, but most careers can become fairly static at their higher levels, and it's then that you start to look round for something else.

Physical movement is very important to you, and for that reason many Arians find jobs involving hard physical work satisfying. It is often said that Arians should be professional sportsmen and women, but openings are few and Arians are many, so many of you have to make do with playing your favourite sports at the weekends.

You're not bothered, when it comes down to it, what you work with; fork-lift trucks or fruit drinks, they're all the same to you. What you're not so good at, though, is working with *people*; to begin with, you're better on your own than in a team or partnership (and you prefer it that way), and secondly you're so direct and positive that you can't understand people who aren't. That's why there are relatively few Arians working in caring and counselling jobs where looking after other people is the main thing.

What Arians do have, which other signs lack, is a talent for working with metal tools. It used to be said, for that reason, that Arians made butchers, surgeons and soldiers, because of the links with blades and weapons, but the range is much wider than that nowadays. Welders, mechanics, any sort of vehicle driver — the list is virtually endless.

To sum up:
- you're best on your own, and on your own initiative;
- you need to be busy, and to be mobile;
- you're good with any sort of tool or machinery.

Things to avoid:
- anything which prevents you from moving;
- anything where you can't do it in your own way;
- anything where other people, and their feelings, are a priority.

People
You like people who are:
- active and decisive;
- able to get on with what they are doing without getting in your way or needing your help;
- honest and open.

You dislike people who:
- tie you down or prevent you from moving;
- are feeble or indecisive, and won't take a risk;
- bother about details;
- deceive you; you're easy to con, because you're so straightforward yourself, and it hurts when you find out.

TAURUS

Home

All of your favourite things are the ones which give you that physical reassurance mentioned in 'Being a Taurus' on page 18. You like furniture which is big enough to hold all of you without you having to perch precariously on one edge of it, uncertain as to whether it will take your weight or not, and you like it to be comfortable. You don't like things which are brutal or ugly, and that includes the shapes of things, too: for you, comfort includes being relaxing to look at.

Everything in your home, all the furniture, all your clothes, all your possessions, all conform to the Taurean design philosophy:

* it must be comfortable;
* it must be of the highest quality I can afford;
* it must reassure me;
* it must look and feel good.

Anything which doesn't meet these four conditions has no place in your life.

Buying presents for you is easy. All anyone has to do is to buy you something which is either beautiful to look at, a treat to wear, or which tastes delicious. What you want is for your senses to be given pleasure, and anyone who recognizes this will have no trouble in finding the right gift.

Cars

Cars are an important part of the way the Taurean likes to show himself to the world. It is something you work long and hard for, and something of which you are very proud. All your possessions are important to you, because they are solid reminders of all that you hold dear. Some signs take comfort in what they've done or what they know, but for you it's what you've got that matters.

The physical appearance of the car actually matters more to you than its performance. You like to be reassured by the quality of its build, the gleam of its paintwork, and by the depth of the carpets. What matters to you is how it feels, and the sensation you get when you sit in it. If the seats are thin, and the trim is all plasticky, you are dissatisfied: you're worth more than that, you think to yourself. So you buy the luxury version, the one with the tweed seats and the extra soundproofing, the one with the smooth ride and the six-speaker sound system. These are the things which give you pleasure and which serve to remind you what a fine person you are, and how much you deserve these little touches of refinement.

You never choose a car which is too thin or too long; they may look sporty or dashing to other people, but they lack the handsome, rather broad proportion that you like to see. You like round cars rather than angular ones, and you wouldn't say no to an estate car, because then you'd have room for all the creature comforts you like to take with you on a journey, like travel rugs, picnic hampers, little folding chairs, six-packs of various drinks, and things like that, which seem to accompany the Taurean when he goes for a drive.

Green is said to be the favourite Taurean colour, and that applies to cars as well. Taureans tend to be Volvo people — the solidity appeals — but whatever you buy, you will walk straight past the red one and the sports version, and head for the green, the white, or the metallic beige, and for the top of the range version with the genuine wood trim — even in a hatchback.

Food

Taureans love food more than any other sign. To you, food is like life itself, and something which provides you with a very deep and lasting pleasure. Most of the other signs just eat because they need fuel, or to be social, but you eat because it answers your very

deepest needs. The most highly developed of the five
senses in a Taurean are taste and touch, and eating is
one way of using both of them at once. The actual
process of chewing and swallowing, or having food in
your mouth and getting the flavour from it, is as
satisfying an experience to a Taurean as running is to
an Arian. The only trouble is that you get some funny
looks when you are asked what your favourite pastime
is and you reply in all honesty that what you like doing
best is eating. Don't feel bad about it, and above all
don't feel guilty. Taureans feed their souls as well as
their bodies by eating, and if the other eleven signs
can't appreciate that, well, that's their problem.

Taureans are fairly substantial people, on the whole,
and so you like your food to be substantial, too. Not just
large helpings, though that is part of it, but food which
is in itself pretty solid. There's nothing you like better
than a good roast, with all the trimmings. All this
designer food, where you get two or three elegant
mouthfuls, is all very nice to look at, but it isn't really
enough for a Taurean appetite. You like to be able to
see what your food is; if it's processed or prepared in
such a way that you can't recognize it, or if it's too far
removed from its natural state, than you're not so keen
on it. This liking for food in a fairly straightforward way
means that you prefer traditional cooking most of the
time. Freshness and quality of ingredients matter to
you, and the way you like to see your food means that if
the ingredients are less than perfect you will be able to
see it at once. You like to see food in its original
colours, too, not hidden in sauces. A plate needs to
have greens and browns on it, the colours of earth and
vegetation, to really please you. As far as flavours and
textures go, you like them to be natural too. You like
your food to have some texture to it — it gives you
something to chew, and that means using your mouth,
which you like — and you like flavours to be as full and
natural as possible. You're not fond of the hot and spicy

food that your Arian or Scorpio friends eat, though, because in your view too much seasoning hides the real taste.

You're not a great fish eater, but you like seafood. Part of the reason for that is that seafood is usually seen as a treat or a special delicacy, and you are a bit of a snob with food; if something is expensive or a luxury treat than you are bound to develop a taste for it, so that by eating it you can remind yourself of how highly you value yourself. Lobster tails, caviar — you like them all.

But all of this is simply delaying that most exquisite moment, when the sweet trolley comes round. All Taureans have a very sweet tooth, and are quite unable to resist anything made with either cream or chocolate, preferably both. It may seem impossible for you to believe, but there are signs who don't like cream cakes because they find them sickly, and who don't eat chocolate because they'd rather not get fat. Amazing, isn't it?

Holidays

Your liking for food extends to your holidays, too. Wherever you choose to go, the food had better be nice or you're not going to like it, even if the weather's marvellous and the sea is warm and blue.

Taureans aren't actually all that keen on beaches and the sea, mainly because the colours are wrong. There's too much blue and yellow to look at, and too much flatness: what you prefer is something with a bit of green or some flowers in it, and some rolling curves like a range of hills. Scenery is important to Taureans: you're an Earth sign, and you get a feeling of being safe and at home when you're out in the countryside, enjoying the scenery.

You don't like touring holidays, either, Taurus isn't a sign which moves around when it doesn't have to, and so what you prefer is to go somewhere pleasant and stay there for a week or two. The feeling of knowing where you are, of feeling at home in place, is very important to you, and you won't get that if you keep moving from one place to another.

Wherever you go, you like to do it in style. Like your taste in cars, your taste in holidays puts comfort and service at the top of the list, and if you have to pay a little extra to get the best then you're happy to do it. Shoestring touring, where you take chances on there being a plane or bus, and where you stay anywhere you happen to be, doesn't appeal to the true Taurean.

There are a number of places which are said to be Taurean in flavour; see if any of them appeal. First of all come Ireland, which is green all over, of course, but if you'd like somewhere a little sunnier, then Cyprus is a Taurean island, according to legends, and so are the smaller Greek islands in the Ionian Sea, and the coast of Turkey, which is a new holiday area.

If cities rather than coasts are more to your taste, then Italy has three famous Taurean towns for you to try: Mantua, Parma, and Palermo in Sicily.

Drinks

Taureans are quite fussy when it comes to choosing a favourite drinking place. What you want is for the bar to function as a sort of home from home, a place where you are well-known, and where you feel comfortable. The sort of place that will appeal to you is one which has a rather old-fashioned feel to it, and which has old and comfortable chairs. You will probably 'adopt' one of these chairs as your own special place, and after a few months the regulars will get used to you always sitting in it. Since you like eating so much, your pub is likely to serve good, traditional food; a Taurean needs more than a bag of peanuts to keep him going. The sort of places that *aren't* Taurean are the modern ones, which have one-word names, and which are fitted out inside with chrome rails and fluorescent lights.

When you're in a pub, you tend to stay in the same

place in the room — somewhere away from the entrance, not too near the back, and out of any draughts. If a few more friends should drop in, you don't suggest that you all move to a larger table, you stay where you are, and then they have to squeeze in as best they can. Once settled, a Taurean doesn't move.

As far as the actual drinks go, a Taurean doesn't like anything too thin or too light. Mr Taurus drinks traditional beers, mainly because they have a chewiness which he finds satisfying. He's not particularly interested in its alcohol content, but he needs to feel *nourished*, and light beers don't give him that. His sweet tooth might lead him to stout or brown ale on occasions. Ms Taurus' tastes are similar, and she may also drink sweet wines or mixtures of spirits and fruit juices; what she's after is something which is sweet and strong at the same time.

Sports and pastimes

Taureans enjoy physical activity, but they're not very fast on their feet. This means that if you want to become a demon squash player or a tennis champ, you're going to have to work a lot harder than everybody else. What you are good at is punching and shoving, and at body contact sports where defence is more important than attack. Taureans are wonderful rugby players, and good defending footballers; you are also good at wrestling and judo, where *holding* is important, but not so good at boxing or karate, where *striking* is emphasized

Being in contact with the earth is good for Taureans, so country walks and gardening will be good for you. Actually, Taureans are the best gardeners of all; you really do have green fingers, and you can make absolutely anything grow.

Taureans have a good ear, and enjoy music both to listen to and to play; they also have the finest voices in the zodiac, and often find that they like singing in choirs or choral societies. But most of all, the Taurean talent lies with colour, shape and material, and the process of making things. Some people regard painting and decorating as only slightly better than having their teeth filled, but as a Taurean, you love the whole process of making a home a better place. Some of you are so good at this sort of thing that you renovate whole houses, and make a large profit when you move; some of you go into the interior decoration business as a career.

Taurean women (and Taurean men, if they would let themselves try it) seem to have a natural ability for handling and working fabrics, and are excellent dressmakers and upholsterers. It's all in that wonderful Taurean sense of touch, you know.

Food, so central to the Taurean existence, can of course be a pastime as well. All Taureans enjoy cooking, and some of you take it very seriously indeed. There are a lot of Taurean chefs and restaurant owners, whose premises are beautifully decorated by Taurean designers, and who serve the finest foods, carefully grown by Taurean farmers. All of these activities are Taurean, and you have a natural talent for anything to do with them.

Colour and style
Clothes are as important to you as they are to anybody, but they have to be pleasing in two ways rather than one: not only must they look good, they must feel good too. That special Taurean sense of touch means that your clothes have to feel wonderful when you feel them on your skin, because you feel them all the time, which other signs don't.

You like very soft fabrics — the softest wools, cashmere, and particularly silk. Silk has been associated with the sign of Taurus for centuries: the reason has long been forgotten, but it is probably to do with its softness.

When you move, you move rather slowly, and you

are a bit heavy-footed, so you shouldn't choose anything which restricts your movements in any way, or you will look rather peculiar as you walk. Nor should you choose styles which are cut very close, or which fit tightly, because to look good in those the body needs to be a different shape to the Taurean frame. Instead, choose styles where there is plenty of fabric, in classic proportion. Taureans look rather grand and dignified in good clothes, whereas some of the other signs look uncomfortable and out of place. It's all a question of making the most of what you've got. Let your hands choose things for you — that Taurean eye for colour and cut, and that magic touch, have a natural ability to pick out the best suit in the shop. The trick when dressing a Taurean is to choose things which have big, soft curves in them, and to avoid straight-cut styles and rigid outlines. That applies to male Taureans, too.

Taureans look particularly good in country styles, where the predominant colours are green and brown and where soft but tweedy textures are much in evidence; you are much less successful in dark blues and greys, or in city styles, where the emphasis is on vertical lines.

Work
Taureans are better suited to working with realities than with ideas, so if you can find yourself a job with a real product, where you are actually making or producing something, you will be happier than working in some administrative function where there's nothing to be seen at the end of the day.

You like to work with your hands, and they are where your talent lies, because as I have mentioned before, your sense of touch is the best in the zodiac. You also like things which are going to last, and things of quality, which are well made; if you're involved in the production of something cheap or disposable you will feel dissatisfied.

A great number of Taureans find themselves working with food, which comes as no surprise since you appreciate it, but there are just as many of you working in the property business, either as estate agents, builders or surveyors. Again, what attracts you is the solidity, the permanence of bricks and mortar, the feel of a good set of walls around you and firm ground beneath your feet. A lot of Taureans like to work with plants — you can get your hands into the earth, you see, and Taurus is an Earth sign, like Virgo and Capricorn — so farming, gardening, fruit growing, landscaping, and all sorts of things like that appeal. Those Taureans who prefer to stay indoors are to be found either in some trade connected with interior design and decoration, or in the fashion industry, where their skill with colour and texture can be used to good effect.

To sum up:
- choose a job with *things*, not with paperwork or figures;
- make sure you're working with things you like; the sort of stuff you'd like to have yourself;
- use your Taurean talents: colour, shape, sound, the feel and flavour of things.

Things to avoid:
- anything which requires speed, quick reactions, flexibility;
- anything which requires you to be hard on other people to make progress yourself;
- anything which requires you to make the first move all the time, and to break new ground.

People
You like people who are:
- considerate and supportive;
- appreciative of your taste and of the things you own,

without being jealous of them;
- careful to stay on their own territory, and not to trespass on yours.

You dislike people who:
- demand, or, even worse, take and use, your things as though they were their own;
- tell you one thing one day, and another thing another;
- try to push you into doing things their way;
- are convinced that they are right;
- tell you what trash most of your prized possessions are; you are *very* sensitive about your belongings, much more so than other signs.

GEMINI

Home
Your home needs to have room for you to move around. It needn't be big, but it mustn't feel at all crowded or dark. You tend to choose light colours for walls and furnishings, though not necessarily white, and you like big windows that you can look out of. You spend a lot of time looking out of the windows: some people use their home as a retreat from the world, somewhere to turn their back on everyone else and sit close to the fire, but a Gemini likes to see what's going on in the world. After all, you know everything that's in your house, because you put it there; but the outside world is full of new things, things you might not have seen before, and you find that interesting. The Gemini love of novelty and variety will never leave you, no matter how old you get to be.

Gemini homes have a lot of books, magazines, and newspapers in them. You love to know what's going on in the world, and you love reading, so it's not surprising. There are probably two televisions, and at least two radios in a Gemini home, so that words and images are available wherever you happen to be. There is likely to be more than one phone, too, unless the house is very small.

Cars

Cars are an essential part of the Gemini lifestyle. What matters to you is that you get to see a lot of people, and that your life has plenty of variety: staying in the same place bores you to distraction. The answer, of course, is to get out and about, and to keep changing the scenery. You'll happily travel by bus or train, and you'll walk if there's nothing else for it, but a car is the real answer. It will take you wherever you want to go, and as often as you like.

If the last sentence sounds too obvious for words, then consider this: other signs don't want cars simply to get them from place to place. They may want them as status symbols, a way of showing how well off they are — Taureans and Capricorns do this, and would much rather have a plush limousine which gets stuck in the traffic than a little runabout which gets them there faster. Getting there isn't so important to them, you see.

Similarly, Cancerians and Pisceans want their cars to be a retreat, a defensive cocoon against the world. When they're out in their cars they feel that they are travelling in a little bit of their own home, safe from outside intrusions.

The only signs which put getting from one place to another, and fairly briskly, in *first* position on the list of things a car should do, are Gemini and Sagittarius. The difference between you is that the Sagittarian is more interested in long journeys; he likes travelling for its own sake and will happily consider driving for hundreds of miles just for the pleasure of it. He may devise some point to his journey, such as seeing a foreign country, visiting a notable castle, or whatever, but what he's really in it for is the journey itself. You're slightly different. Most of the time your trips are short ones, and in fact you dislike long journeys, because your quick Gemini mind gets bored doing the same thing for too long, and you find yourself wishing you were there already. What you travel for is to see people and to talk to them, and too much time spent travelling means less time spent talking. What you want a car to do is to speed up and increase the number of social contacts you have in a day.

So which car do you choose? Something small, usually. The Gemini mind never thinks that bigger is necessarily better, and if a car's size is likely to slow it down, then you don't want one. Little cars, which can go through narrow gaps, and which can find a parking space that others would have to pass by, have a lot of appeal for you. Little cars also have light controls, usually, and that's something else you like; Geminis don't enjoy hauling on heavy steering or fighting a temperamental gear lever. Some signs do — it's part of the game to them — but you want things to move with no more effort than it takes to think about them.

Unlike the signs which regard cars as status symbols, you don't care whether it's the latest model, or whether it's new. What matters to you is what you can do with it, so price isn't a consideration. Old cars are fine as long as they run, and you never find yourself gazing longingly at the advertisements for the performance saloons and wishing you could have one. You'd much rather have a little Gemini car to zip round to see your friends any time you like.

Food

Food isn't the most important thing in a Gemini's life. You like it well enough, but if you really want to understand what food *can* mean to somebody, then talk about it to a Taurean.

As usual, what you're after is variety. That means food which is attractive to you, and which will entice you into wanting to try it. You're not the sort of person who will eat the same thing every day; if you were to do that you would know what it was going to taste like, and then you'd have no need to eat it because there'd be nothing to discover about it. That should show you something about your eating habits — you eat from interest, not from hunger or habit.

You quite enjoy meal times, but you dislike eating alone. The reason isn't hard to find — it's the Gemini need for mental stimulation again. When you're eating in company, there are people to talk to, and you enjoy that. You also enjoy the fact that when other people are eating they're usually in a good mood, so the conversation is more agreeable. As you can see, the food itself comes second as far as you're concerned.

Buffets are ideal for Geminis. Not only can you eat and talk at the same time, and to a number of people on the same occasion, without appearing rude, which is wonderful for you, but you can also eat lots of different things, so that you get that variety of tastes which always pleases you.

Your favourite foods are all rather light. You like light meats, like chicken, but are less fond of heavy steaks and roasts, probably because you get bored with all the chewing. You like spicy flavourings, but not necessarily hot ones, and you particularly enjoy anything which has two flavours at once, like sweet and sour sauce. As ever, you're after variety.

Variety in the colour of the food, and clever presentation also attract you because they excite your interest and curiosity, and that's what's required before your taste buds start to work. You find yellows, oranges and light browns attractive in food; left on your own in front of a huge buffet table you'll go for the chicken and sweetcorn salad because the colours seem right.

One thing you don't do is overeat. Gemini is a fast-moving sign, and you like to feel light and springy, ready to move; you can't do that if you're too full of food, and so to avoid being too full you simply don't eat much.

Holidays

You like holidays. You even like thinking about holidays, and planning them, because there are so many places to choose from and you like comparing this place with that, and this hotel with that, and so on. You never get flustered by having too wide a choice; when you've got 50 different things to compare against each other, all different, you're as happy as you can be.

A Gemini holiday isn't two weeks on a beach turning brown, though, it isn't even two *days* on a beach turning brown. As ever, you want variety more than anything else, so you try to find somewhere that you've never seen before, and where there's a lot of different things going on. You like busy towns with plenty of street life rather than sleepy little villages, and you'd much rather be in a real place, where real people live and work, than a purpose-built resort where the only inhabitants are other holidaymakers.

What you like is to be nosy about other people's business. What do they do for a living? Where do they have their lunch? Above all, what are they saying to each other, and to you? You couldn't be happier than to be in a bar on a busy street corner in Italy, listening to the daily chatter of all the regulars, or to be in a crowded market somewhere in North Africa, watching farmers haggle over the produce they've brought in from the surrounding hills. Geminis have a distinct interest in trade and bargaining, which the other eleven signs don't; if there's a deal going on, anywhere, you like to watch it, see what the outcome is, and if possible to be in on it as well.

You need to talk to people, so if the people where you are don't speak your language then you'll learn theirs — it's as simple as that.

There are a number of places in the world which, because of the date of their foundation, or discovery, or whatever, are associated with Gemini, and are said to have a Gemini character. You might enjoy some of them. The largest by far is the United States; that constant drive towards newer and better things disturbs some signs, but to you it all makes perfect sense. London is a Gemini city, too, a constantly changing centre of trade and communication. In Europe, the Lombardy region of Italy, around Milan, is Geminian, and so is the island of Sardinia, according to tradition. Finally, two fine Geminian cities: Cordoba in Spain, and Nuremberg in Germany.

Drinks

Pubs are one of your favourite places. It's nothing to do with the alcohol, it's to do with the social life. As usual, what you want out of anything is mental stimulation and variety, so you enjoy any place where people gather and chat.

When you're in your favourite pub you usually sit to one side of the main thoroughfare, not tucked away in a corner somewhere. What you want is to be able to see what's going on. If anyone new and interesting comes in you want to be able to see them, and to see what they're doing. You don't necessarily face the door, but you're usually facing towards the bar, because that's where the centre of activity is in a pub, and activity creates interest, for you.

Your interest in trade and exchange gets some exercise in a pub, too, and you enjoy that. There is usually somebody in a pub doing a deal with somebody else, or selling something, and there are often games of darts or dominoes going on. All this sort of thing interests and amuses you, and it's part of what you go to a pub for. You're not interested in playing games on your own, and you'd much rather not be drinking on your own; social contact is the magic ingredient in everything for you and without it life seems dull.

Your taste is for light drinks on the whole. You're not interested in a drink as a form of nourishment, as

Taurus is, and you're not primarily drinking to get drunk, so the alcohol content needn't be very high either. The reason you have a drink in your hand is as a ticket to join a conversation, and nothing more. Miss Gemini has a taste for very fizzy drinks, though she may change as she gets older. The Gemini liking for variety stays, though, and so Guinness can be a Gemini choice, because it comes in two colours.

Sports and pastimes

Gemini is a sign of movement, and so you need exercise to stay at your best. More than the other signs, you need to move your arms and shoulders around, yet you don't need anything which requires a great deal of strength because you don't have either the build or the aptitude for that sort of thing. You also need social contact, of course, to give you somebody to talk to, and so those sports or games where there is no other player or partner can't really give you all that you want. Finally, you need mental stimulation; you get bored if there isn't something to watch and think about, something fast-moving to make you concentrate.

The perfect answer to all these requirements are the racquet sports — tennis, badminton, squash, and so on. Badminton is possibly the best of them for you, because of the sense of lightness and airiness which the game has: lightness and grace of movement are closer to the Gemini soul than sheer speed and power.

Racquet sports require the player to be light on his feet, and to change direction quickly, yet not to have to go very far when he moves. All of these are the very things which Geminis have a natural ability for, and which need exercising if you are to stay fit and well.

Racquet sports are also two-player games, and often organized in clubs, where there is a social element as well, thus meeting every Gemini need.

There are lots of Geminis who enjoy dancing, too. It is the mixture of movement and choreography which

appeals, occupying the mind at the same time by
concentrating on light, but accurate, footwork.

Light but accurate *fingerwork* is what interests
Gemini musicians. They like instruments with keys, and
those which have a light sound. Woodwind appeals,
especially the flute.

The most common Gemini pastimes are those
involving words, either solving puzzles and
crosswords, or writing. Geminis love words, and they
love making sentences in their heads. They also love
the physical process of writing, making words appear
on paper with a pen, and they are the only sign which
does. You love playing games, too, of all varieties, and
you love playing for money, even if it's only for a few
pence.

Whatever a Gemini does to amuse himself, it is
characterized by having light but intricate limb
movements, and a much greater mental effort than
physical one. Precision is important, and always you
will choose fine work rather than heavy. You would
rather take a watch or a radio apart than strip a truck
engine. If you get good at whatever you do in your
spare time, you will start to earn money at it; that
Gemini love of trading, of doing deals, is never far
away.

Colour and style

Geminis never wear too much of the same thing. Even
if you have to wear a dark suit to work, with a dark tie
and dark shoes, you will find some way of showing
some contrast, some variety. You much prefer to wear
separates, clothes which go together, but which are
quite different, and which can be used in different
combinations, something you haven't seen before.

For the same reasons, you don't like plain cloth,
either; you'll always pick the one with a pattern of some
kind, either in the weave, or in the dye. You don't like
big patterns, though. If you look around your wardrobe,

you will find that there's nothing with a really big motif on it, and nothing in wide stripes, either. Narrow stripes there should be plenty of, because you're rather fond of those, and small geometric patterns or prints, too. You're also fond of checks; other signs think they're loud, but you think they're lively and amusing. It's the variety you're after, the combination of different colours and patterns.

Everything you wear has to allow you to move, and it must be light. You don't like heavy coats — indeed you may not have one — because they seem to weigh you down so, and you always like to feel light and mobile. Jackets have to be big at the shoulder and in the sleeve, to allow you all the arm movements you like so much, and you seldom wear a jacket fastened, because it restricts your upper body movements.

You don't like dark colours, either, and only wear black when you have to. You quite like grey, especially in its lighter shades, and you brighten it up with flashes of colour from scarves and things like that. You also like yellow and light browns, and greens, if they're not too dark; you tend to stay away from reds and blues as a main colour.

Work

Work and play have to be the same thing, to some extent, or you won't do it. What you want your work to offer you is a mental challenge which is tough enough to make you feel that it's worthwhile, easy enough for you to be able to do it within a reasonably short period of time (which can be as long as a few weeks, but certainly not months), and something which is never quite the same twice, so that there's something new each time. If you can find all that, which isn't easy, then you will be delighted, and the time will fly by; if you can't, then you will become dissatisfied and bored, and you will look for something else to fill your time with, doing less and less of what you are supposed to be doing. Eventually you will leave the job because you can't see why you should still be there if you have no interest in it.

As you can see, how well you do depends *entirely* on how interested you are. If your career doesn't develop, it isn't because there are better people than you, or because you can't master the intricacies of the job, it's because you've lost interest.

You like to think that you could move at a moment's notice if you wanted, and that means not having responsibilities. Most jobs acquire responsibilities as they develop, but Geminis cleverly steer clear of as many of them as possible — not because you can't give what's required, but because you'd rather not. You don't want to feel tied down.

Gemini jobs are light on labour but heavy on brain-power and words. There are a great number of Geminis who are attracted to journalism and radio, where words are the major medium, and there are plenty of Geminian teachers and lecturers, too. The computer industry, especially software development, is ideal for the Gemini's puzzle-solving mind. So is any form of buying and selling, from the Stock Exchange to a market stall. It's all to do with communication, movement and exchange.

Even these jobs are too static for some of you, who have to be on the move all the time; you'd rather be postmen or delivery drivers, who make lots of short journeys, and see a lot of different people for a few minutes each working day — very Geminian.

To sum up:
- your progress up any career ladder depends on how much the job captures your imagination;
- you have a talent for anything involving words, or buying and selling;
- find a job which tests your ingenuity, not your stamina.

Things to avoid:
• any job which is unchanging or repetitive;
• any job which has heavy responsibilities for other people and their welfare attached to it.

People

You like people who are:
• bright, talkative, and funny;
• up-to-date, excited about the latest thing;
• not too upset if you change your mind or don't feel like doing something, even if you promised earlier that you would.

You dislike people who:
• take every word you say as absolute truth, never to be altered, and who correct you later when you say something different;
• have no sense of humour, and don't talk much;
• have deep emotions, and expect a similar emotional response from you.

CANCER

Home

A Cancerian home is a retreat from the world. You are safe there, and you can do as you please. Some homes are for public view, in that they are designed and furnished to impress or accommodate a visitor, but your home is *private*. It's the inside of your shell. It's the place where you can take off the suit of armour you wear all day, made of good manners, good behaviour, shyness and tidyness, and stand it in a corner while you flop in a chair and unwind.

Your home is full of your personal things, collected over the years, and each with a special memory or a story attached to it. You can't bear to part with anything, so your home is filled with all sorts of stuff. Some signs don't ever seem to collect anything — Aries is one —

while others catalogue them all neatly, or throw away all but the most important or most impressive. Cancerians keep the lot.

Cars

To a Cancerian, a car is a device for moving from one place to another in safety and privacy. There is a certain similarity between a car and the crab of the sign: both of them have hard outer shells, rather roundish in shape, soft interiors, and the means of movement underneath, such that when they move, the larger outer shell stays upright.

The idea of the car and the crab being similar will not be new to you, even if you haven't been able to put your finger on it exactly before now. People buy cars which resemble them — or, more precisely, which resemble the way they imagine themselves to be — and since you are a Cancerian, you are likely to buy a car which has Cancerian virtues.

Cancer, like all the Water signs (the others are Scorpio and Pisces), likes to feel protected from the outside world. You're a private sort of person really, and rather shy; you wouldn't like everybody to feel that you were public property, or for total strangers to treat you as though you were old drinking partners — you'd be very upset. Nor do you want your feelings to show to anybody until you've known them for a while and feel that you can trust them. So for all of these reasons, you don't want your car to tell the world anything you'd rather it didn't know. That may seem rather an obvious thing to say, but the other signs are quite different to you; they'd love to show the world how proud they are of themselves. Fire signs (Aries, Leo, Sagittarius) are always doing this. These are the people who have loud red sports cars, the ostentatious limousines, the oversized four-wheel drive pick-ups which only collect groceries from the supermarket car park. *Their* cars get their owners noticed, something which you, as a

Cancerian, would rather avoid.

The inside and the outside of your car are likely to be very different. You are likely to choose something which looks fairly solid from the outside, but you don't want it to be at all hard or basic on the inside; you want comfort and convenient features instead. It's just the same as the crab, with its hard shell outside and soft creature inside, and you yourself, with your shy, reserved exterior, and your warm, caring interior.

Home is somewhere you feel safe, and free to do as you please, and since your car is your home while you're on the move, you make its interior a room of your own. Cancerians are untidy creatures at home (which is odd, considering how well-behaved and proper you are when you're in company), and it won't be long before your car fills up with little personal bits and pieces, too. Some signs take all the petrol vouchers and toffee papers out at the end of each journey, you know: Virgos do, for instance. Not you, though.

When you're buying a new car you read all the road tests, like everybody else, but while they're looking at the performance and the horsepower *you're* checking to see if all the windows are made of safety glass, and whether the seats recline. As ever, security is your first priority, and then comfort. Your choice is always responsible, considerate. You think of the other people who will use the car, particularly your family, and you put their needs before your own, often. You would never let yourself buy something completely impractical, useless except as a part of your personal fantasies.

The sort of shape that appeals to you is a rounded one; straight lines, or anything pointed, put you off. Cancerians were very fond of Volkswagen Beetles when they were around, and you still have a soft spot for Volkswagens generally, because they have a reputation for safety and reliability which appeals to you. For similar reasons, you like Saabs — especially the older ones, which again have a rounded, Cancerian shape. Truly round cars are hard to find nowadays, but the latest large Fords are nicely rounded and suitably crablike, so perhaps one of those might appeal. Your colour preferences are for the colours of the Moon, Cancer's own planet — silver or white.

Food

Cancerians have one or two specific likes and dislikes in what they eat, and you may be able to spot them in your own favourite dishes. To begin with, you don't like food which takes a lot of eating: big pieces of meat which need determined chewing aren't to your taste at all, and neither is anything with an irregular texture. *Smoothness* is what you like; your favourite foods are often those where the ingredients have been beaten and blended very finely: mousses and pâtés, things like that. You like creamy desserts, too. Cream seems to feature in a lot of your favourite food, but it isn't so much because of its richness or flavour — though that's why Taureans love it — but because of its smooth consistency. You love cream sauces: if you're dining out somewhere expensive for a treat, your eye is always drawn to those dishes on the menu which have light meats (chicken, veal, fish) cooked in cream sauces. Meat which is light in colour is particularly suited to the sign: Cancerians and red meat or, worse still, game, don't go together so well.

Cancer is a Water sign, of course, and so you need lots of water to function properly. Plain, pure, water is the best drink for you, and plenty of it; the mineral and spring waters which are so popular now are excellent for Cancerian well-being.

Most of the food which is best suited to you, and which you like, either contains a lot of water, or originally came in water. By this I mean fruits and salad vegetables, which are full of water, and of course fish.

And finally, there's one food which is always associated with the sign. It is mostly water, it comes in a

Cancerian colour, and it has Cancerian associations of
mother and family, too — milk.

Holidays

What a Cancerian wants most from his holiday is a rest.
You don't want an all-action fortnight of constant parties
and social life, you want somewhere quiet and peaceful
where you can feel that there's no pressure to do
anything.

As always with a Water sign, there has to be water
around for you to feel completely relaxed. Most
holidays have water in the form of the sea, but in fact
more suited to the Cancerian soul is stiller, quieter
water, such as a lake or a canal; a week of lakeland
scenery will be more relaxing for you than a week in
some busy resort.

The eternal problem with the Cancerian on holiday,
though, is the fact that you'd rather be at home,
surrounded by the things that you know best. Being in a
strange environment means that you have to familiarize
yourself with everything around you before you can
start to enjoy yourself, and that takes time. For many
Cancerians the best answer is to take your home with
you, as you do, for example, in a caravan or a camper
van.

Another way that Cancerians make a home from
home is by going on self-catering holidays, where the
chalet or villa becomes home for a week or two.
Somehow you just can't switch off your home-making
instincts and let someone else do it all for you, can you?

Probably the best answer of all for a Cancerian
holiday is to live on a barge, on a canal, for a couple of
weeks. Peace, quiet, water, home from home, it has
them all.

Canals feature in one or two of the world's Cancerian
places, too. Zodiac signs are given to places according
to the date of their foundation, or discovery, or
whatever, and the towns or countries labelled thus do

seem to show the qualities of their signs. Perhaps you would enjoy visiting a place associated with your sign.

Holland is reputedly a Cancerian country, and so is the city of Amsterdam, which has lots of canals. Italy isn't Cancerian as a whole, but Venice is, and again, it has canals. So does Stockholm, which is also said to be Cancerian. Not every Cancerian city has to have canals, though: Milan and New York don't, for example.

Cancerian places have something of a reputation for rain. Scotland is Cancerian and so is Manchester — but so is North Africa, which is a bit of a puzzle, but perhaps the weather was different in Roman times, which is when it was given its zodiac sign.

Finally, a tropical island for the Cancerian who wants to be a long way from anywhere, and to listen to the ocean: Mauritius. It has plenty of sunshine, of course, but it gets plenty of rain, too, so you'll soon feel at home.

Drinks

Cancerians are usually happier to have a few friends round to their house than to go out to a pub. It's all to do with feeling safer in familiar surroundings, as usual. When you do go out with your friends, you're not usually the one who is the life and soul of the party; you prefer to sit quietly and watch all the fun. One thing that Cancerians seem to do, though, and your friends will tell you if you do it, is to put yourself right next to the person who is the centre of attention. They shine all the more brightly for your being there, and *you* can have a good time without feeling that you're expected to take the lead or put on a performance in any way.

As far as choosing a pub goes, your favourite is one with a single large room rather than lots of small ones — that way you can be part of the crowd and yet still part of the action. You also like to sit with your back to the wall, because it means that nobody can creep up on you from behind. You do that in restaurants, too; you won't eat where you can't see who's looking at you.

Your choice of pub is also likely to be one you've visited before: familiar surroundings again. You don't like a place that's too modern, but you don't like one that's too dark, either: for a Cancerian, it must have a traditional flavour, and be comfortable, yet be quite light in feel.

As far as actual drinks go, your tastes are modest. You need the liquid, like all the Water signs, but it's the Scorpios who like strong flavours, and the Pisceans who like alcohol for its own sake. You're happy with a half pint, or even a soft drink. When some of your friends start to fall over you'll laugh along with everyone else, but you won't let yourself get into that state, at least not in public; you're more reserved than that.

Your one alcoholic weakness is a cocktail with cream in it. The wonderful smooth texture of something like a White Russian is irresistible to you, and it's about the only thing which will ever tempt you to drink more than you should.

Sports and pastimes

The obvious recreation for a Cancerian is something to do with water. What you're looking for in your sport is not the explosive action and muscular activity which, say, the Arian needs, but something which will occupy your body in a smooth and flexible way whilst allowing your mind to stop worrying for a while. You need to undo all the tensions which everyday life puts into your body, and to unravel your mental knots, too. Messing about in boats has always been a favourite Cancerian pastime, and so has fishing. The quiet sitting by the river bank is probably more appealing than actually catching anything.

There are such things as active Cancerians, but the most satisfying activities are still the ones with water in them. Sailing can be quite energetic if you want it to be, and water-skiing is good for those Cancerians with Fire signs rising (see page 219).

Among the more strenuous pursuits, Cancer has always been associated with wrestling, whereas boxing goes to Aries, or so the Ancient Greeks reckoned.

Away from the playing field or the ring, Cancerians choose hobbies which are linked to their family life, or to the planets associated with the sign. Knitting is apparently a Cancerian craft, and perhaps other forms of needlework, too. Cooking, and doing things around, and to, your home are also Cancerian, though there's a lot here which is shared by Taurus, the other great home-loving sign. *Extending* your home, for example when you build an extra couple of rooms on, or convert part of the building into something else, is definitely a Cancerian activity.

On a more artistic level, Cancerians enjoy things made of glass or silver, and may well collect items in both materials. Silversmithing has always been associated with the sign. Something more modern which has associations with the sign is photography; not only does it enable a moment and its emotion to be kept, something very dear to the Cancerian heart, but in addition the active ingredients in the photographic process are salts of silver. Isn't astrology neat?

Colour and style

Cancerian dress sense is different from that of the other eleven signs. What motivates you is not whether a garment is practical or suitable or even fashionable, but what it reminds you of; the major force in Cancerian dress sense is *sentiment*.

When you buy something new, you are quite likely to try to find something very similar to what you already have, the idea being that if you liked the old one you will like the new one, and that the new one will remind you of how good the old one was each time you wear it. It's not a bad idea, but it means that you tend to stay with styles which are increasingly dated just because you like them. Fashion goes in cycles anyway, and the water signs' styles are 'in' every 20 years or so. The last time was at the end of the 'Seventies, so you may well find that some of the most treasured items in your wardrobe come from that era.

Cancerians have to be careful not to look too messy; you have a talent for untidiness which can ruin your best attempts to look smart, and you're not the sort of person who can get away with wearing too many things which don't match, or which have fussy detail. Leave that sort of thing to Geminis and Librans. Something else you have to guard against is that all your outfits start to look the same after a while; no matter what colour or cut they had originally, they begin to resemble each other. It's very odd, and only Cancerians can do it.

Dark colours don't suit Cancer, on the whole; the colours of the signs are white and silver, and while it isn't always possible to wear them, you do look better in lighter colours. You also have a dislike for styles which achieve their effect through sharp, abrupt lines; you prefer a jacket with soft, rounded shoulders rather than one with a squarer cut, for example. The same goes for shoes, too — you like traditional styles, and rounded shapes.

Work

Cancerians have a talent for looking after things, and especially for looking after *people*. That's all there is to know about your work and your career; you may say and do a great deal more, but at the end of it all, you are a *carer*.

What you are particularly good at is understanding the feelings of people as they work, and the various unspoken rules which establish who is in control, and what's important. You can take over a whole network of people and processes, and make sure that they continue *exactly* as they always have done. There are no changes, no problems, no hurt feelings. What's important to each individual becomes important to you, and you make sure that every little thing gets the care and attention it needs. Nothing gets forgotten or brushed aside.

Your real talent is for dealing with people. A lot of people prefer to deal with bits of machinery, or numbers on a page, or money, because these things are fairly predictable, and they don't answer back; human beings, on the other hand, are all different, and quite unpredictable. You much prefer human beings; they have a warmth and a vulnerability which brings out the best in you. Cancerians care what happens to other people, and willingly give time, effort, and sympathy to anyone who needs them.

For this reason a great number of Cancerians find themselves working in the caring professions, nursing, advising and helping those who are ill or in trouble. Teaching, especially young children, is another area which attracts you.

Some of you work in museums, archives, and libraries: you're caring for the past, keeping caring for the work of past generations so that future ones can enjoy it. All very Cancerian.

Cancer is always connected to the house and home, so a lot of you find yourselves attracted to working with property and housing. Whatever you do, the jobs which appeal to you most are the ones connected with Cancerian values of stability and care; very few Cancerians like working with anything which is simply produced for a quick profit and nothing else.

Although you have tremendous talents for caring and general management, it's worth knowing what you're *not* so good at. Firstly, you find it hard to be an entrepreneur, to feel your way as you go along, and to make progress by the force of your own conviction and some lucky timing. It's too risky for you, and you would worry too much. You're not an original thinker, either; what you're very good at is picking up somebody else's idea and making it better, but the original thought doesn't come from you.

Secondly, although you're quite prepared to give all your time to someone in trouble, you need them almost as much as they need you; without human contact you wither away. You need a job where there are plenty of people around you, however much you may think the opposite.

To sum up:
- you're at your best when looking after people, or being a manager;
- your talent is for understanding, sympathy and care;

Things to avoid:
- any job which requires you to come up with new ideas or ways of working;
- any job which has no human element in it.

People
You like people who:
- are sensitive and sympathetic;
- have a feel for the value of things in human terms, and especially of anything delicate or needing special care;
- respect authority, position, and privacy.

You dislike people who:
- are rude or nosy, intruding into your private thoughts or feelings;
- are deliberately selfish or unhelpful;
- threaten the security of you and those you care for.

LEO

Home
Leo homes are palaces, which is only to be expected from the royal sign. Only the best is good enough for

you, and at home you like to be able to remind yourself of how fine a person you are, especially when the world has been giving you a hard time.

There's nothing in your house which is small and dainty; in your eyes, such things are too small to be useful, and liable to be broken. Your taste in furniture is traditional, but *large*; you like an armchair to be big enough to settle into without worrying about whether you are going to overbalance or not, and you want the upholstery to be comfortingly luxurious. The only snag with all this is that it is difficult to find homes these days with rooms big enough to furnish on your sort of scale, so to some people your house can look a bit crowded. It isn't, of course, it's just that when you've got a banqueting table *and* a grand piano in a modern room there isn't a lot of space left. The same goes for your taste for gold-plated or brass ornamentation; it only looks wrong because your imagination is sometimes larger than your house.

Cars

A Leo's car is one of his favourite possessions. You like to look at it, you like to drive it, and you like to be seen out in it. It says something about you, reminding both you and the rest of the world what sort of a person you are.

This price of ownership is something which the Fire signs (Aries, Leo and Sagittarius) and the Earth signs (Taurus, Virgo, and Capricorn) have in common. The other six signs don't want their cars to say anything about them — and in the case of the Water signs (Cancer, Scorpio, Pisces) then the less you can tell about the owner from the outside the better it is!

That's not *your* way, though. You want the world to be able to see you, and to notice you, and if you thought your car was going to pass unnoticed in the traffic, then you'd rather walk. That's because your personality is so big; you have far too much energy and warmth to keep it all to yourself, and so you like to share it with whoever happens to be around. You're proud of yourself, and you don't mind who sees it. And the same goes for your car.

What you need in a car is something big enough to show the size of your personality. Small-minded and unimportant people have small cars, you reckon, and because you're a generous, big-hearted soul, you'll need a big one. Room to feel comfortable, and to spread yourself and your things around in. You'll never choose anything small, no matter how good the arguments for inexpensive running and easy parking, because you simply can't function on a small scale — it cramps your style, and you feel crushed, emotionally as well as physically.

Grand cars, as in Rolls-Royces, Cadillacs and the like, have always rather appealed to you. For one thing, they're big and roomy, and for another, they stand out in the traffic, so that everyone knows you're there. The fact that they're very expensive doesn't impress you all that much. Leos aren't after status in that way, because they *accept* it as part of the way that they are. Every Leo knows that he is one of the finest people ever created, and has no real need to prove it. The sign that loves to show how expensive a car it can afford is Capricorn; to a Leo, the price is a secondary consideration.

Comfort is something that you and Taurus want out of your cars. You like the seats to be large and comfortable, all in leather if possible. You like things like armrests on the doors, and in the middle of the rear seat; and you like wood-and-leather fascias rather than cold grey plastic. Electric windows are the sort of swanky toy which takes your fancy, but digital instrumentation, or too many engine function monitors, annoy you. Leos aren't interested in the engineering side of things; you're in it for the pleasure of driving.

Above all, what you want your car to be is a proper

reflection of you, and your own natural importance. People as fine as you are hard to find, you feel, and so to reflect this accurately you must have a car which is equally rare. That means that most ordinary cars, no matter how well-appointed, aren't suitable for you, and you won't even consider them. There are simply too many of them around, and that's that. The top of the range executive cars are approaching your standard, but it all depends whether anyone in your street has already got one; you won't let yourself copy someone else — Leos are unique, after all. Japanese cars are out of the question, because Leos have a preference for things with some history and tradition attached to them, a sort of aristocratic flavour which attracts you.

At the top of your list stand the hand-built grand cars of long tradition, the Rolls-Royces and the Bentleys. The true Leo would actually choose the Bentleys, of the two, because Leos are Fire signs, and Fire signs are active and sporty, and they do things themselves. Even if you have a limousine, you'll still drive it yourself, because it's something you enjoy doing. Bentleys are generally seen as being slightly sportier than Royces, more active, more approachable; closer, in fact, to the character of the Leo — and that will tip the balance of your choice.

Not everyone can afford such things, though, not even every Leo. Further down the price range, but still with all those Leonine qualities which the world needs to see from you, is the Jaguar, which generations of Leos have loved over the years. And smaller still? Peugeots, possibly; after all, each one has a little Leo lion on the front, and you could hardly resist that.

Food

A liking for good food and a hearty appetite is something a Leo shares with Taurus and Scorpio. Fire signs are the zodiac's meat-eaters, and that includes you, of course. Aries is probably the greatest meat-eater of them all, but you run him a close second, and vegetarian Leos are rare animals indeed, just as there aren't any real lions which don't eat meat. The traditional big meal, centred on a handsome roast with all the trimmings, is a Leo's idea of his dinner; a couple of sandwiches or a few mouthfuls of salad just aren't enough to keep you going.

With an appetite like that, you're going to become quite solidly built, and most Leos get rather round in middle age. Dieting is miserable for you, though, so you don't bother with it, on the whole. You do have one advantage over Taurus, however, and that is that you don't have as much of a sweet tooth as he does; it's probably what saves Leos from becoming seriously overweight.

Whatever you eat, it has to be of the finest quality. Other signs have chops, but Leos prefer fillet steak; other signs have cod, but Leos prefer salmon. And so on. It's all to do with the idea that you are what you eat, and since you firmly believe that you are of the very best, then your food must match.

The best thing about the way you eat, though, is your liking for eating in company. You love to have a big meal with your family and friends around you, and before you know it, what started as lunch turns into a party. That's Leo eating at its best — good food, good company, and a good time for everybody, not just for you. Leo *shares* his enjoyment, and makes life fun for others; that's why everyone else in the restaurant just can't help joining in.

Holidays

Leo is the sign of the Sun, in astrological language; isn't it typical for your sign to be given the brightest, warmest, most important thing in the sky? Of course it is, though it's the other way round, actually — Leos are the most important people because they are associated with the Sun, not the Sun given to the Leos. Anyway, you love the Sun, and so your idea of a holiday is to go somewhere where you can be under its golden beams most of the time. More than all the others, yours is the sign which likes to lie in the sun and just soak up all that bright warmth. The other signs only do it because Leos do it, you know, but they're nothing like as good at it as you are. You're the Sun's sign, and you're better in the warmth than the other eleven signs. You also tan better, and you know it.

Although you like to laze around all day, you do like some sort of entertainment in the evening; a sleepy little resort where there's nothing going on isn't quite what you want. All Fire signs like activity, and so they choose places where there's plenty of social life, and lots to get involved with. The Arians actually want to be busy all day, so they choose holidays which centre round a sport or something like that, while the Sagittarians want to see interesting local sights, and to get into the local way of life. Leos are a little more laid-back than that, preferring to take life more or less horizontally during the day, but by the time that the sun's gone down in the evening your batteries will be fully charged, and you want to be in lively surroundings.

The countries of the world have zodiac signs, too; horoscopes aren't just restricted to people. It's usually said that if you go to a place which is said to have the flavour of your sign, then you'll enjoy yourself more, because you'll feel more at home. As usual, Leos get the best bits of Europe, and the sunniest bits, too. All of France and Italy are said to be Leonine, which is probably why you enjoy the riviera lifestyle so much. If you really want to chase the sun, then you could try Israel, which is also Leonine.

Finally, a few Leonine cities for you to try. Rome and Ravenna share your sign, as you might expect, being in Italy, but so do Chicago and Philadelphia in the USA, Prague in Czechoslovakia, and for the real long-distance traveller, Bombay.

Drinks

The good time that you have when you're eating travels with you when you go to the pub. Leos are among the world's great socializers — Aquarians, the sign opposite you, are the others — and you're likely to be both a welcome and a familiar sight in your local. That sounds obvious, I know, but some signs aren't really social drinkers: Cancer and Virgo, the signs each side of your own, are good examples.

When you're in the bar, you like to stand in the centre. There are some people who always sit in the corner, and some who stand near the door, but even if the place is packed by the time you get there, you'll fight your way to the centre of the room and make yourself some space there. There is no point in being anywhere if you're not at the centre of things, in the Leo view. It might be that your friends are already there, sitting round a table — in which case you'll either take the best place at table, and make the others move round to suit, or stay standing in the middle, and wait for them to join you. Either way, you get to be at the centre of the activity, you always do things that way — it's just how you are, and nobody seems to mind.

Leos are generous to their friends, and that means that you get to buy a lot of drinks for people, but you don't mind in the slightest, your own taste is only for the best. When you're eating out, you drink the noblest wines, and when you're in a pub, the best beers the house can offer. A typical choice for you might be Löwenbräu — its quality, reputation and price are all very high, and there's a golden lion on every bottle, which is sure to appeal. Older Leos often become fond of spirits, especially double scotches (the double is important! Leos always work on a large scale).

Even in a cocktail bar, the Leo style is unmistakable. What you like are the drinks which are famous for producing a good time; with that in mind, and the fact that Leos have a curious affinity with citrus fruits, is it any wonder that you find yourself ordering a Harvey Wallbanger or a Tequila Sunrise?

Sports and pastimes

Leos aren't actually the world's greatest athletes for the most part, there's too much running about involved, and you're always careful not to do anything which might make you look silly or undignified. You quite like playing games, though, at a fairly gentle rate, so a bit of weekend cricket or tennis might appeal. You don't have the Arian's love of using his body, or the Sagittarian's rugby-club fondness for all getting sweaty and filthy together, though you do like the social aspects of a sports club. What makes you take up a game is as likely to be the sort of people you meet there as anything else, and so you'll join something like the golf club.

Leos are tremendous part-time workers for good causes, and it's not unusual for you to spend your weekends doing something fairly frivolous to help a local charity. Part of the reason you're so good at it is because you're so good-natured and generous, but you're a good organizer, too, and it shows.

Something else that you love doing is taking part in any kind of show. Acting, or anything theatrical, is something which comes naturally to Leos. You're so good at this sort of thing, in fact, that you're quite likely to do it semi-professionally; once you've found something you can shine at, you do it so well that you're no longer really just an amateur. The same applies to painting, and the Arts generally — Leos are full of creative talent, and it's just a question of finding the right outlet for it.

Colour and style

Leos are the sign the other eleven wish they were. No matter what you wear, or how you wear it, you always manage to look terrific. It's probably to do with the fact

that you always have bags of self-confidence and that
you always walk very upright, with your head held
high.

Yet in spite of this model-like posture, you're one of
the slowest to adopt new trends, and a lot of your
favourite clothes are rather conservative in style. Why
is this?

It's to do with not wanting to make a fool of yourself,
something you never forget, though nobody would
ever guess it. You'll wait to see whether a new style or
a new shape settles down into mainstream fashion
before you'll be seen wearing it, and you'll also wait to
see whether it becomes established at the upper or
lower end of the market. Leos, whatever their position,
always dress *up*.

The most distinctive part of a Leo physique is the
upper torso, and it is an essential part of Leo style to
display or emphasize this. A few years ago the way to
do this, for male Leos, was with an open shirt and a
gold medallion (gold is Leo's metal). More recently,
female Leos have been able to emphasize the Leonine
shape with the fashion for wide and padded shoulders
in jackets and blouses.

As with everything else, your choice in clothes is
more expensive than that of the other signs, because
you are matching what you wear to your opinion of
yourself. One thing that Leos don't suffer from is an
inferiority complex! You enjoy expensive fabrics, and
you like your clothes to be quite heavy — unlike, say,
Gemini, who wants everything light and airy, and who
almost never wears a coat. You are also the sign which
is most likely to wear fur; perhaps the Leo doesn't feel
complete without his mane.

The most easily identifiable part of your personal
style, though, is your liking for gold. Leo men usually
have at least a gold ring and a gold watch, while Leo
women have everything possible: rings, chains,
bracelets, and much more.

Zodiacally speaking, Leo should prefer to dress in the colours of the Sun — yellow, orange, gold — but your unwillingness to look odd means that Leo men, in particular, are unlikely to do so. Instead, Leos choose *royal* colours like rich reds, blues, and burgundies.

Work

Leos can sometimes have trouble in choosing, or finding, a suitable career. The reason is extremely simple, but arriving at a solution to the problem can sometimes seem impossible.

The reason is this: the natural position of a Leo is that of number one: the topmost, the person in charge, or the most important. As you can see, you will have no doubts as to which direction you should aim in, but it isn't easy to get to the top almost as soon as you start, and it's the waiting which is going to be difficult for you.

What you have going for you is your talent for organization, and your cheerful manner. There is something about Leos which makes them natural leaders, and when you find people coming to you for advice and direction, which they will, then make the most of it. The more you are seen as the sort of person who can direct others, then the sooner you will get to that position at the very top which is where you belong.

What you're not so good at is being one of a team, or even worse, one of many in a large department. If you find yourself in a situation where you're lost in the crowd and ignored, then either you're going to get very depressed about it, or you're going to misbehave in some way so that everyone will notice you. Both of these are unhelpful to you in the long run, so the only answer is to move, and put yourself in different surroundings with a different job.

For many Leos the only answer is to work for yourself. Lots of Leos are craftsmen or performers of some kind: the link between what looks like two totally unconnected areas there is that they both require that individual creativity which Leos have so much of.

The traditional career roles for Leos have always been those of director, financial manager, and so on. Leos are indeed excellent administrators, and perfectly suited for life at the top, but not every Leo can be a managing director. Whatever you do, though, it must give you some degree of control over the way things are run, and it must give you an opportunity to show how having you in charge is in fact the best thing for everyone, not just yourself!

To sum up:
- You're good at anything which needs an organizer;
- You're better as a big fish in a small pond than the other way round: don't be tempted to join a large, important, Leo-sized organization unless you're sure that you will get to the very top.

Things to avoid:
- Anything which gives you no room to move;
- Anything where you will be on your own, without much personal contact;
- Anything where the end product is either invisible or uninspiring.

People
You like people who:
- are generous in spirit, and laugh a lot, like you;
- are pleased to be in your company, and show it;
- are the best in their field, whatever they do.

You dislike people who:
- try to upstage you or prove how much better they are than you;
- are all 'take' and no 'give';
- won't take time off to relax and have fun once in a while.

VIRGO

Home

Virgo homes are, understandably, neat; everything is in
its proper place. Your taste in furnishings is rather old-
fashioned, and there is an emphasis on *separateness*,
which works like this; rather than have a three, or four
or even five-seat sofa unit, which occupies all of one
wall and half of another, including the corner, you have
a number of chairs. That way each person has a chair
to *themselves*, one person on a seat for one. Another
reason why you prefer chairs is that they tend to be
taller, or at least appear to be, than sofas; vertical
dimension appeals to you, and the extended shape of a
three-seat sofa seems too flat, somehow, to be right for
you.

As with your choice in clothing, your choice of
interior decor often includes some small, but regular
pattern, such as stripes, or a small floral print. Your
mind is restless; it needs to be interested by things, and
the patterns are there because they are more
interesting than plain colours. For the same reason,
your house is likely to have a fair number of books,
magazines, and little objects which you can pick up and
play with when your hands and mind need something
to do. Your best collection of little objects to play with is
actually in your kitchen, where there are likely to be
such things as a cherry stoner, or a thing for slicing
beans. To most people, these are delightful gadgets
which they would never think to use; to you they are
essential tools which enable you to do specific jobs in
the best possible way.

Cars

Virgos aren't the sort of people to make a great fuss of
their cars. Before you protest that you are very fond of
your car, and that it cost a great deal of money,
consider this: Is your car the most important thing in

your whole life? Probably not. Yet for some signs, particularly Aries and Scorpio, and probably Capricorn too, the answer could well be 'yes'. For them, their car is more than a means of transportation; it's a larger version of themselves, on show to the world. You're not like that: to you, a car is a machine. You may be very proud of it, but you're never likely to confuse it with yourself.

Virgo is an Earth sign, like Taurus and Capricorn, and all the Earth signs are looking for the same sort of qualities in their cars. To this group of signs, what matters is the quality of the thing itself; how well it is built, the fine materials used in it, the craftsmanship and the prestige. Earth signs, you will notice, care about the car's *physical* qualities; you wouldn't buy a car which had rust showing through its panels, or which didn't run very well, no matter what it was. Fire signs, like Aries, would buy a red sports car simply because it was a red sports car; the fact that the doors might not close properly is of no importance to them. What matters to them are the car's *dynamic* qualities. And what matters to signs like Libra and Pisces is how it looks, rather than how it goes.

Still, it's the physical qualities which interest Earth signs, and that means you, of course. Your Earth sign companions the Taureans are the ones who really appreciate the materials in their cars, enjoying such things as leather seats and walnut dashboards, but Virgoans are impressed by something else; it's the craftsmanship and the quality of manufacture that you find most satisfying.

For you, a car has to be *perfect*: perfectly assembled, without a loose bolt or a frayed wire; perfectly designed, so that nothing is inconvenient or difficult to use; and perfectly reliable, so that everything from the engine to the courtesy light in the boot gives years of fault-free service.

Virgos place a great deal of emphasis on the use of

their hands, and of the feel of things. You don't like anything which sticks into your hand, when it could have been made more rounded, or anything which is stiff or awkward when it could have been designed to have a better action. If something like that annoys you, you're the sort of person to take it apart and alter it so that it does what you want it to. Lots of people — the other eleven signs — never give a moment's thought to the way the indicator switches or the door locks work on their cars, but Virgos do, because you always notice details, and the way things work matters to you.

With this famous Virgoan perfectionism comes a sense of cleanliness and lightness, of clear and accurate vision. Needless to say, you won't ever buy a car with a dirty interior, and you won't buy one where your view of the outside world is spoiled (in your opinion) by a high bonnet line and small windows, either.

Dark colours aren't very Virgoan, and black certainly isn't, so those cars which surround the driver with great expanses of soft black padded fascia full of dials and switches don't attract you. You like the information the dials give you — the more information the better, you think — but you prefer them to be set in something like pale grey or another light, neutral colour, and you also like the dashboard design of cars to contain more straight lines than circles, if you see what I mean.

Finally, what you like in a car is what the designers call 'thoughtful touches'. Individual interior lights, seats which adjust for height as well as reclining, that sort of thing. As long as they all work perfectly, of course. And two great luxuries, which mean more to you than all the go-faster engine tuning in the world: power-assisted steering, because of the lightness of touch it brings to the whole process of driving, and air-conditioning, because Virgos are *extremely* fussy (some would say obsessive) about breathing clean, fresh air.

The car of your dreams, the one which you would

buy if money were no object, is probably going to be a Mercedes. The quality of manufacture and the attention to detail are very Virgoan indeed. Further down the price range, Virgos find Japanese cars attractive; the favourite is likely to be Honda, whose combination of high reliability, light controls, clean design, and lots of 'thoughtful touches' has a strong appeal.

Food

The same qualities that govern your choice of car — quality, neatness, cleanliness, proper function — are also to be found in your choice of food. Virgos have something of a reputation for being fussy eaters or health food freaks, and it's worth seeing how this comes about.

What actually happens is that you try to ensure that the food you eat is of the highest quality. You don't like to think that you could have done better — either in the quality or in the cooking and presentation. It follows from this that the finest quality foods are usually fresh ones rather than canned or frozen, and so you tend to eat things which are as unprocessed as you can get them. As you can see, if you do this you are going to be eating a lot of fruits and salad vegetables, and very few 'ready meals' from a packet. This is how Virgos get their reputation for being fussy eaters. It isn't fussiness at all; it's just a search for the highest possible quality.

A lot of Virgos are vegetarians, and there are a number of possible reasons for this. The one which is most often put forward is that you are trying not to clog up your body's systems with heavy foods and chemical additives, but it may equally well be true that you have an aversion to gravy. Sauces of all kinds are difficult for Virgos to handle properly; not only do they disguise whatever they're poured over (Virgos hate things to be *indistinct*), but they add to the general mess on the plate, and mess is something that offends your sense of neatness and order. Messy food, or food which is difficult to eat, is really too much for you if your Virgoan characteristics are very strong; spaghetti bolognese is definitely not your idea of fun.

Doing things properly, and doing things neatly, are an essential part of your Virgo-ness; things which can't be eaten neatly, or which you don't know how to do properly, like eating with chopsticks, perhaps, will bother you — especially if you're out in public.

Natural food is what you like best; plain cooking, lots of fruit and vegetables, and no junk food at all. To you, food isn't about giving in to your sweet tooth, being social with your friends, or even about flavour; it's about *nutrition*, and that's something you take seriously.

Holidays

What you are popularly supposed to want from a holiday — blue skies, hot sunshine, a beach, a tan — aren't really on your list of priorities at all. Earth signs like to see the Earth looking lovely, and a string of holiday hotels crammed together next to a flat strip of sand doesn't have what you're looking for. Hills, and trees are what you want to see: *greenery*, in fact, some sort of evidence that the earth is capable of growing things. Taurus likes to see rolling hills and green pastures, whereas Capricorn likes to see high mountains and jagged peaks; Virgo is somewhere in between.

The most Virgoan country in Europe is supposedly Switzerland. It has the perfect blend of high mountains and green farmlands, and it has a brisk, clean flavour which is very much to your liking. And, of course, it has the cleanest, freshest air in the continent, something which means a lot to you.

You need to feel that a holiday does you some sort of active good, that you come back from it better than you went. Lazing on a beach for a fortnight may be relaxing, but to the Virgo it feels too inactive; you'd like to be doing something which is refreshing you, exercising you, making you healthier.

A lot of Virgos go on cycling holidays, and in mountainous regions, too; it's the efficient, healthy use of your energies that you like.

When you do choose to have a beach holiday, for whatever reason, the Virgo choice is for the Eastern Mediterranean rather than the West. The island of Crete is supposed to have Virgoan affiliations, and so is Northern Greece; perhaps it's the combination of the famously clear air and the rocky scenery which attracts you.

'Virgoan affiliations', meaning that a place is considered to have the flavour of a zodiac sign, isn't just limited to a few rocky islands. There are several cities which are connected to zodiac signs, and it seems that Virgo has more than its fair share of the world's most beautiful places. Both Paris and Lyons in France are Virgo places, and so is Heidelberg in Germany. Across the Atlantic, Boston is a Virgo city, while Norwich claims the sign in Britain. A holiday in any of the cities of your sign is sure to delight you.

Drinks

Virgo taste in drinks is a little out of the ordinary. To begin with, there are plenty of Virgos who don't drink at all, usually for the same reasons as those who don't eat meat. Those who are left fall into two broad groups: the real ale drinkers and wine snobs, and those who like their drinks very dry.

The first group are the sort of people who care about how their drink was made, and what its got in it. The more skill involved in making the drink, the more you like it. Something which is made of the finest ingredients and produced entirely by hand will be more to your liking than something which has been made in bulk at some anonymous factory. For this reason the Virgo drinker cultivates a taste for obscure real ales rather than popular lagers, and for wines which come from small estates rather than cheaper, blended products. This is often seen as a sort of one-upmanship, but it isn't; once again, it is simply the pursuit of high quality ingredients and hand-crafting, which mean so much to you.

The second group are those who simply drink for the flavour of their drink, Virgo taste is very plain, very straightforward, and doesn't usually include sweet things. As a result you choose drinks which are clean, clear, pale in colour, and dry in taste, and a good example of all these things together can be seen in your favourite cocktail: the Martini. A Martini has to be made properly if it is to be any good at all, and that's the whole point — what you're looking for, as ever, is something which is done properly, and done well.

Sports and pastimes

Virgos enjoy physical exercise, but they don't enjoy direct competition, so team games or games for two players like tennis, aren't as popular with the sign as some people might think.

The most popular Virgo sports are those where the body movement is regular and rhythmical, and where one of the benefits is fresh air; walking of all kinds, especially hill-walking, is of great benefit to Virgos, and so is cycling, Virgos have a special fondness for the bicycle: it suits the physique of the sign, and its clean and efficient mechanical simplicity have a direct appeal to the Virgo mind.

Away from the playing field, Virgos take up all sorts of interests to keep busy. Partly this is because you have an enquiring mind, and partly because you don't like to sit still and do nothing. But over and above all that, Virgos have the most wonderful talent for any craft or manual activity, and a gentle patience with materials, such as wood, which can make them do almost anything you want. Lots of people like to decorate their own houses, but Virgos can make their own furniture as well. Like your zodiacal relatives the Geminis, you have a facility for fine mechanical work, such as mending electrical things, or clock and watch repairs, which often leads you to pursue your hobby semi-professionally.

Colour and style

Virgo style can be summed up by using four words: small, classic, neat, subdued. If an article of clothing cannot be described by using at least one of those words, and preferably more, then it is not the sort of thing a Virgo would choose.

Different signs of the zodiac have different colours associated with them, and people do tend to choose the colours of their sign. Virgo's colours are dark greens, dark blues, and greys. There is an old astrological tradition which suggests that you might like a splash of yellow now and again, but such times are few and far between. What Virgos *don't* wear is red; they leave that to Arians and Scorpios.

What you *do* like is small patterns; you are the sign most likely to choose something with a little print motif, or a very narrow stripe, or little dots. Everything that you choose by way of a pattern will be small, but a little bit of decoration pleases you more than a plain colour.

The styles you choose are usually very neat and tidy. You don't go for flamboyant clothes, or anything too exaggerated; very wide shoulders, or a very revealing neckline strike you as being rather silly, so you don't wear them. What does attract you, and which you like to wear, is anything which shows cleverness, either of cut or construction, and anything which shows the skill of the person who made it. Absolutely perfect double stitched seams are the sort of thing you like to see.

You keep your clothes as good as the day you bought them, too, and you have the magic ability, which the rest of us don't have, of looking as neat and clean at the end of the day as you did when you started. Sometimes you show off this ability by choosing combinations like navy and white — a Virgoan favourite — and keeping both colours spotless and unmarked, which is beyond the capabilities of the other eleven signs.

The only problem you have with clothes is your shape. Virgos are rather long in the middle, and most clothes don't have their waist in the same place as yours. Perhaps because of this, you choose styles which enable you to leave the waist area undefined. Check through your wardrobe and see!

Work

Virgos have a much easier time making a career for themselves than some of the other signs, and the reason for this is that you have talents in two large areas which can always be put to use.

The first one, which was always the area in which Virgoans were always traditionally employed, is anything requiring a particular manual skill. Any trade which required the working of wood or metal, or any detailed assembly or painting, was ideal for the Virgo's patient skills. Nowadays there are fewer opportunities in those areas, but the Virgo's eye for detail and analytical mind finds plenty of work in the growing computer industries, and in electronic engineering in general.

The second Virgo talent is quite simply for noticing things. This is most valuable in any sort of quality control, or any process where inspection and the maintenance of high standards are involved. It takes a particular sort of mind to check apparently identical rows of figures on a page, or wires in a circuit, and see which one is the faulty one, but that's precisely your talent, and there is no shortage of people willing to employ it.

There is one other area which the Virgo has virtually

made his own, and that is public health, in all its aspects. Virgos find it easy to extend their concern for their own well-being to that of others, and there are many ways of doing it. There are Virgos working as dentists (lots of them; it's a fine hand craft, and a way of helping the health of the public at the same time), in clinics for just about everything, as public health inspectors, in the preparation of food, and in all sorts of related areas.

To sum up:
- You're good at anything which requires observation and skill, less good at jobs which require sheer strength
- To be at your best, you need your work to be small, and for each job not to last too long
- You work better on your own than in a team

Things to avoid:
- Anything which is administrative rather than productive
- Anything which deals with large scale operations: you get lost in the size of it all
- Any process dealing with ideas rather than actual objects.

People
You like people who:
- Appreciate the practice and the dedication required to make something difficult look easy;
- Are prepared to do what is right and for the best, even if it's not what they themselves would like;
- Think before they act.

You dislike people who:
- Wilfully damage things just for the sake of it;
- Value things by their price rather than their worth;
- Live in a world of 'airy-fairy' ideas, and never seem to consider their responsibilities and commitments.

LIBRA

Home

Libran homes are light and airy, as might be expected. They are also very comfortable, and there is almost nothing with sharp edges or corners; contours are gently rounded.

Most of your furniture is soft and comfortable, intended — and used — for being lazy in. The larger pieces of furniture are likely to be rather low in outline, with low backs and low arms perhaps, giving an emphasis on the horizontal lines of everything rather than the vertical. High, straight furniture seems somehow too spiky for you, even if it isn't really like that.

Your colour preference is very much for lighter, neutral shades, like peach, or white; dark furniture, and the deep-coloured fabrics which generally go with it, are not to your taste.

In spite of your liking for comfortable furnishings, the decoration is never overdone in a Libran house, and the overall effect is always very attractive. This is entirely due to your own intuitive sense of balance, which makes you leave as much space empty as there is space full of furniture, and put a picture here, a lamp there, so that the overall effect is always perfectly balanced. Your house is attractive to look at, comfortable to be in, and an ideal place for sitting with friends and talking. Which is, of course, exactly what you want it to be.

Cars

As with everything else they own, Librans get into a relationship with their cars. Yours probably has a name, like 'Bessie' or something like that, and quite often you will make up a name from the registration letters, so that NJL eventually becomes 'Nigel'. It's all done so that you can feel that you're being friends with your car, and it's rather endearing. Many car salesmen have had the experience of the Libran who buys a particular car, no matter how unsuitable for the purpose, simply because the combination of headlights, radiator grille and bumpers make an appealing 'face'. Appearance is actually the most important thing to the Libran car buyer, and you are quite likely to buy something which looks pretty, or is in an attractive colour, even if it doesn't run terribly well — in marked contrast to a Virgo, who demands mechanical perfection but doesn't pay much attention to the shape or the colour.

It all depends on what you want your car for, of course, and different signs have cars for different reasons. Librans want cars to *do* something, whereas some of the other signs want them to *be* something. The Taureans and Capricorns, and the Virgoans too to some extent, want their cars to show the world how well-established and wealthy they are. For these people the price tag and the luxurious fitments matter far more than the car's looks, or how rewarding it is to drive; and indeed, some of these cars are never driven at all — they simply sit in the drive and look impressive.

Librans, however, are not like that. What you want is for the car to be fun to drive, and for it to fulfil two purposes; firstly, to take you to see your friends, and to keep you socially active, and secondly, to take you and your closest partner anywhere you want to go together.

You will notice, I hope, that the motive behind all this is social communication, the process of seeing people and talking to them. This is what Air signs (Gemini, Libra, Aquarius) do best, and what you *need* to do if you are to stay healthy. Your car, therefore, must make it easier for you to do this; if it doesn't, it's the wrong car.

What you like in a car is for it to be light and mobile. Librans are always light on their feet, and graceful in their movements, so if your car is heavy and clumsy, you won't like it. Cars which have low seats and a low roof, but high doors, so that you appear to sit enclosed in a dark cabin and to peer out through narrow windows, are not your sort of thing at all. The next sign on, Scorpio, will love all that, but it's not airy enough for you, and you find it closed in and depressing. Cars which are very long, or very wide, or which aren't very manoeuvrable, aren't to your taste either; you're looking for something which can almost dance into a parking space, and which can slip effortlessly through gaps in the traffic without a second thought. Finally, your own hand and body movements are light and fluid rather than heavy and forceful, so any car which needs a strong foot for the clutch or a firm hand for the gears gets low marks from you, too.

Actually, your insistence on lightness and airiness, plus your irrepressible romantic streak, leads you to consider a type of car which is almost a Librán trademark: the convertible. Whether it is the airiness which attracts you so much, or the Libran togetherness implied by a car which can only hold two people, is difficult to say, but you love soft-tops. So much so, in fact, that you don't mind the heavy controls and bumpy ride that some of the older models have, as long as it's a convertible and it looks good.

Looking good is something else which matters to a Libra, as you probably know by now. Little two-seat sports cars are often very eye-catching, and that's another point in their favour as far as you're concerned. You're very taken with cars which have graceful lines, too; Librans find curves more pleasing than straight lines. A lot of modern cars are rather angular, made up of straight lines and wedge shapes, and one reason why you still have a fondness for old two-seaters, despite their hard ride, is that their style is much softer and more curved.

When it comes to choosing a colour, you're fairly

flexible, as long as the overall appearance of the car is light and bright. It is rare for a Libran to buy a black car, though (much too dark), and unless there are other influences in your horoscope to suggest it, you're unlikely to buy red, either. If you had to express a preference, it would probably be for white.

So what will you choose? Twenty years ago you would have had a white MG convertible, but they're getting hard to find nowadays. Perhaps the closest to the Libran ideal at the moment is a white Toyota MR2 sports car. A Golf convertible might tempt you, or maybe a Peugeot 205; in fact, there are plenty of Libran cars around at the moment, because all of the neat and nippy little hatchbacks, most of which are available in white, have something of the young, friendly, romantic Libran ideal in them.

Food
Lightness and sociability, those two threads which run through everything you do, are there when it comes to food as well. Some signs — particularly Taurus — take food very seriously, because it gives them the same sort of satisfaction that being in love gives you; in other words, it answers an emotional need as well as a physical one.

The air signs, however, of which you are one, you will remember, think of eating as something to do *in company*. To you, dinner is an opportunity for a social gathering with added food, and not the other way round.

You don't like long meals, or rich and heavy food. This could be because you prefer things light and simple, but it could also be that having to pay too much attention to the food prevents you from talking as much as you'd like to.

More than for any other sign, the visual aspect of food has a great influence on whether or not you eat it. For you to even consider it, it must *look* appetizing first. That means, for Libran taste, that it must be light, bright, and colourful. If a dish is dark in appearance, or is all the same colour, it won't appeal to you. What you're looking for is variety and balance; some of this balanced by some of that, so that nothing is too heavy or too much for you to eat. Nor does a large plateful appeal to you — Librans have rather small appetites.

Your favourite kind of meal is probably some sort of a buffet. It has everything you could want. You don't have to eat a lot of the same thing, and best of all, the meal is designed so that you can continue talking to people while you eat.

Favourite foods for your sign are said to be the light meats — veal and pork, say, rather than beef or game — and of course chicken. Turkey is also supposed to be specifically Libran, though nobody seems to know why. One thing that you do have though, is a sweet tooth, something you share with the Taureans, since both of you are born under the signs of Venus, and Venus is associated with sugar and with sweet flavours. Put your liking for attractively presented food together with your sweet tooth, and the result is a passion for cakes; and since you also like light things, it's a fair bet that one of your favourite treats is something like a meringue.

Holidays

There's little doubt about what you go on holiday for. It isn't the sun, and it isn't the sea; it's the social life. The holiday romance is a Libran invention.

Some people go on holiday to get away from it all, and they're so serious about it that they go away on their own, so that they don't have to spend any time with anyone they know.

You can't understand that. You like to go on holiday in a group, with a party of friends, or at the very least with one other person; if you went on your own you'd be completely lost — until you found somebody to spend your holiday fortnight with, which might take you several minutes once you'd arrived. You simply can't function without other people, and a holiday is no exception.

Although you like being in a group, you're not keen on holidays where everything is organized. The idea of being told what to do seems heavy and inflexible to you, and you like your movements to be lighter and more fluid than that; it's your Air-sign airiness coming out again. You'd much rather be free to do what you want, as the mood takes you. And yet, for all that, you are the person *most* likely to do absolutely nothing but laze in the sun. You should go on holiday with a Leo, who really does like the sun; you would stay in the same spot on the beach together for the whole fortnight.

In many ways, you are the easiest person to take on holiday, because you will always be happy to do what someone else suggests. If everyone is going to the bar, you're happy to go too; if they're going out on a little trip, then that's fine by you as well. It's part of that social impulse that you have, picking things that you'd like instead of disagreeing, and it makes you a very amenable partner.

There are a number of places in the world which are supposedly Libran, and they might appeal to you as holiday destinations. All of Austria is Libran, and so are the Alpine regions where France and Italy meet; they sound ideal for skiing holidays. If you want somewhere sunnier, then Lisbon, in Portugal, is a Libran city. Further afield is China, traditionally a Libran country, but if you simply want to sit and chat in a café, eating your favourite cakes, then you can't beat Vienna, which is a Libran city in its own right as well as being capital of Libran Austria.

Drinks

Your attitude to drinking is the same as it is to eating; that is, it's quite a nice thing to do while you're socializing. For this reason, pubs are popular places with Librans, but Librans aren't necessarily popular with landlords, because they don't drink as much as, say, the Piscean.

You tend to stand in bars rather than sit, because once you've sat down you're likely to stay in the same place, and that stops you from being as mobile as you'd like, and it also stops you from moving from one conversation to another, which is what you really like. The only exception to this is when Libran laziness overcomes your urge to move, or when you have found somebody really interesting, and you want to spend the evening in a one-to-one conversation with them which ignores everyone else present. Wherever you stand or sit, it's in the centre of things; other signs are happy to sit quietly in a corner, or try to find a place where nobody else can see them (watch Scorpios do this), but you like to be at the centre of the social activity.

Your famous Libran indecision comes out when you're ordering drinks. You think you know what you want, but when you get to the bar there are all sorts of other drinks that you can see, and you have difficulty deciding which one you'd like. You can think of good reasons for all of them. Libra always sees two sides in a question, and the good points of both of them. On the other hand, when it's somebody else's turn to buy the drinks, things are a lot easier. You usually reply that you'll have what they're having, and you're happy with that, too — it's that Libran knack for finding points of agreement again. It's best for everybody, therefore, if you don't go to the bar, but get somebody to do it for you.

Your preferred taste, unsurprisingly, is for drinks which are light but quite sweet. You prefer lagers to heavier beers, and when drinking cocktails tend to go for mixtures of light rum and fruit juices, Bacardi and anything, basically.

Sports and pastimes

That famous Libran laziness keeps many of you from
playing any sort of strenuous sport at all regularly,
though your natural talent for supple movement gives
you an advantage in many cases. What Librans don't
have, though, is great strength, or the capacity for
continued physical effort, and if you choose a sport
which requires those things, you will have to make
more effort than everyone else.

Games for two players, such as tennis and the other
racquet sports, are best suited to the Libran
temperament; team games, such as football, are less
so. Best of all, from your point of view, are those games
where the social life is as much fun as the game itself,
like golf.

Most of the time, Librans choose their pastimes to
balance their working life, so that, for example, if their
daily work is noisy, their weekend pastime is quiet.
Quiet pastimes are popular with Librans, with reading
and listening to music as favourites. One notable
exception is dancing, which all Librans love, probably
because you're good at it. With the talent for movement
that the sign gives you, it's not hard to see why.

Colour and style

Librans have an advantage over the rest of the zodiac,
in that they look wonderful in whatever they wear. Most
of looking good comes from moving well, and you do
that naturally; but you also have an instinctive eye for
colour and line which tells you what looks best on you.
Some signs will take a liking to a certain colour or
feature, and wear it to excess, but your Libran sense of
balance always lets you know if what you're wearing is
likely to be over the top, and stops you looking as
foolish as the rest of us sometimes do.

As ever, those Libran catchwords *light* and *bright* are
the key to your style. You don't wear as many clothes
as the other signs; you are the last to put on a heavy

coat in winter, the first to wear light cottons in spring. You don't like dark colours, either. Black has almost no place in your wardrobe, unless you wear it *balanced* (Libran word again) with an equal amount of white. Browns and grey earn your disapproval, too. You are traditionally supposed to favour blue, and it is true to some extent that you almost never wear large amounts of red, which is the colour of your opposite sign, Aries. You are also said to be fond of pink, and you are probably the only sign which can wear the colour well.

Very fancy or heavily decorated clothes are something else that you can get away with, and often rather like. Everyone else drowns in the riot of colour and fabric, but your light step and attractive movements make them work in the way they were intended. Movement, and the ability to make your clothes move, is essential to you — you look terrible in things which restrict your movements, for this reason, you tend to choose styles which are loose, or which have plenty of room for movement, and which are in soft and flexible fabrics rather than anything heavy and stiff.

Work

In choosing a career, Librans tend to fall into two groups; those who want to be involved with something light, bright, and attractive to look at; and those who want to be involved with the process of balancing two sides.

In the first group come all the things which most people associate with the sign. There are painters and decorators, tailors and dressmakers, hairdressers, beauticians, and of course models. All of these are concerned with the business of making something either better than it was before, or with presenting it in its best possible way. None of these professions are usually classed as being 'heavy', and most of them offer a clean working environment along with plenty of variety. All of these are strongly attractive qualities to the Libran. Librans who work in offices work better if the work is varied, and if there are people to talk to. The slightest suggestion of darkness or heaviness can depress you.

The second group is more difficult to define, but is just as important. What it uses is the Libran ability to relate to all sorts of people at a moment's notice, and to act as a go-between, if necessary, when there is conflict. In this group go negotiators of all kinds; counsellers and consultants, diplomats, and lawyers. Here, too, are people who work with people, such as personnel workers, and those whose job is to be helpful and welcoming, such as hotel staff. As with the other group, this group is also interested in presenting a smiling and friendly face, in occasionally difficult circumstances, which is the very essence of Libran-ness.

To sum up, things to go for:
- Any job where the end product is attractive to look at
- Any job where you are the link between two sets of people, such as manufacturers and customers
- Any job which keeps you on the move rather than tied to the same place and the same routine.

Things to avoid:
- A dark and gloomy workplace
- Working either on your own or in a very large group; you're best with a partner
- High-pressure jobs with a furious workrate; Librans don't have the necessary aggression.

People
You like people who:
- are talkative and amusing;
- sentimental;
- attractive to look at.

You dislike people who:

* are too fussy and critical;
* try to force you to do things;
* are unfair to others because of their own selfishness.

SCORPIO

Home

Scorpio homes tend to be rather dark, and densely furnished. That doesn't mean that they are either dirty, or badly lit, just that you like to feel the room closely surrounding you, unlike Librans and Geminis, who like their rooms light and airy.

You go for dark colours, and for heavy and luxurious fabrics. A Scorpio home is sometimes *too* rich — like eating too many soft centre chocolates at one go — and can overwhelm the visitor.

Your taste in furnishings is actually a close match for your taste in clothes: deep, dramatic reds are a frequent choice, and so is black. You are the sign most likely to have leather furniture. The truest expression of your taste, however, is probably in your bedroom, where you give free rein to the passions that you normally keep in check.

Cars

Scorpio cars are usually impressive. They are impressive on both sides, too; they promote a feeling of envy or excitement in other people, who see them from the outside, and they give a feeling of superiority and security to their owners on the inside as well.

To understand how this effect comes about, you have to think about what the sign of Scorpio is, zodiacally. Scorpio is a Water sign, one of the group of signs that consists of Cancer, Scorpio and Pisces, and all the Water signs are characterized by a need to ensure their own security. The Fire signs and the Air signs never worry about what might go wrong, because they are too busy thinking about how fine life will be when they succeed, but the Water signs worry about their own security quite a lot.

It follows from this that Water signs will choose a car which provides them with a sense of security. It needs not only to get them from one place to another as they wish, but also to get them there in *privacy*; when a Water sign person is in his car he is safe from the outside world, and nobody can get at him unless he wants them to. If you like the car becomes a shell, or a cocoon, to insulate the driver from everybody else who crowds around. This is one reason why a lot of Water sign people like to be on their own in their car when they can, unlike the Air-sign types who love to pack in as many friends as they can.

The idea of the outer shell is a familiar one to Cancerians and Scorpios, because the animals representing the signs both have hard outer shells to their bodies, and those born under that pair of signs develop a sort of hard shell to their personalities to match. You can see now why cars which are advertised as being very protective, such as Volvos, might appeal to Water signs. Cancerians do find them attractive, but they lack the special qualities which the Scorpio is looking for.

Scorpios are different from the other Water signs in that they are more intense, more powerful, more concentrated in every way. Everything a Scorpio stands for is impressively, frighteningly, potent in its effects, and of course this intense quality has to be found in the Scorpionic car.

As a Scorpio, you are familiar with, and indeed need, a powerful emotional response from other people. You know what you are doing, and you use it to control them, in a way. If they hate you, admire you, or adore you then everything is fine; but if they are indifferent to you then you can't get a handle on them, and that worries you, to make sure that you get your own way in the traffic, you choose a car which states in no uncertain terms that its owner has power. At the same time, however, you want it to state that the owner is hidden, unknown, mysterious. Put these two requirements together and you have a dark sports car, which is the vehicle most Scorpios say they would like.

In shape, you like things which are rounded rather than long or angular, and you're not fond of bits which stick out or are chromed; smooth, untouchable, dark power, slightly threatening, is what you're after.

Your favourite colours are the colours of the sign: black and red, in that order. Both of these colours have a definite effect on the minds of people who see them, and it's that effect that pleases you.

Your dream car is probably going to be a black Porsche 911 with wide wheel arches and a spoiler on the boot. It even *looks* like a scorpion: black, shiny, menacing. The combination of its contours, its colour, its quality of build, and its performance are a perfect representation, to you, of the power and security which are so important to you. The interior is just what you want, too; the low seats and the predominantly dark-coloured fitments give a seductively sensual feeling which matches your inner moods.

Not every Scorpio can afford a Porsche, but whatever you choose, you will find yourself wanting the performance version, especially if it's in red or black. So, too, does anything long, low, and generally sharklike in appearance, as many of the Japanese sports coupés are. You particularly like them when they have tinted windows, which adds that extra air of mystery. You'll never choose anything which is either slow, pale in colour, or which has a sensible, family-style image.

Food

Scorpio tastes in food are a combination of two factors: being a Water sign, and being under the astrological influence of the planet Mars, which the sign of Scorpio is.

Being a Water sign means that you like your food moist, and that you like it rather soft, too. All dishes which come with a sauce or some other liquid dressing appeal to you. It might be because they disguise the dish to some extent, and you love all mysteries and subterfuge, but the prime reason is because it helps you eat it. Food which is eaten dry, or which needs a lot of chewing, isn't to your taste at all.

Smooth-textured food, whether savoury like pâtés and soufflés, or sweet like cream desserts, is something you like very much. It's probably something to do with the sensations it produces in the mouth as you eat it. Eating is something done more with the tongue, rather than the teeth, in Water sign people.

Water signs are supposed to like food which comes in water to begin with — that is, fish, and all varieties of seafood. You are very fond of seafood, it is true, but fish on its own has quite a light flavour, and you would really prefer something stronger. This preference for strong flavours comes from the influence of Mars.

Mars governs all hot or spicy flavourings, and any foodstuff which is red in colour. This means that you will enjoy anything like curry or chili; the flavour is hot, but the texture is soft, the way you like it.

The combination of these two influences is found in the uniquely Scorpionic experience of aphrodisiac food. Any food which has a reputation for being luxurious and seductive — such as oysters, or lobster — you enjoy immensely, and eat whenever possible. Whether this is because of the flavour and texture, which are usually soft but rich in the way that you like, or because of the effect it arouses in other people, is hard to tell. There is probably a little of both in it.

Finally, Scorpios drink quite a lot, as all Water signs must, to keep their body fluid levels correct. Mars' influence gives you a liking for strong spirits, though: brandy is usually considered the Scorpionic favourite.

Holidays

Scorpios have distinct tastes in holidays, you are the only sign, apart from Aries perhaps, which actively wants to go somewhere where there is an element of risk and excitement, where you might get yourself into a bit of an adventure.

The idea of lying on your back for a fortnight turning slowly brown doesn't appeal to you much, though you like to be in places where the sun is hot. Heat and passion, two of the attributes of Mars, are what you like to experience on holiday. The social life on a beach holiday might give you some of the passion you're after, but not all: you'll still need to find something different to challenge your abilities, and you'll also need some time to be on your own, away from the crowd.

Water sports are something which attract you, which isn't surprising for a Water sign. The ones which you like best are the ones which have some element of danger in them, particularly *underwater* sports, where there is not only the thrill of exploration, which you love, but deeper satisfactions also, which are to do with being under pressure, in all possible ways.

There are various places in the world which are associated with the sign of Scorpio, and which are supposed to have a Scorpionic character. Most of the North African coast is traditionally given to Scorpio, which should provide you with plenty of places where the sun is as hot as you would like it to be. And there, too, you can play Indiana Jones in the crowded markets and narrow streets. There is a strong attraction between Scorpios and Arab culture, which is all to do with the influences of Mars again; you find its passion and mystery very appealing.

Drinks

Like all Water signs, Scorpios enjoy drinking, but unlike their colleagues the Cancerians, they also enjoy using bars as places to watch, and possibly meet, new people.

Scorpios enjoy pubs which are dark and intimate, with all sorts of hidden little corners and alcoves where you can sit unobserved. You're much less comfortable in a modern pub where the walls are cream and the carpet is a light brown, and where the ceiling seems a long way away; what you like is the feeling of being enclosed, tucked away, almost.

Some people walk straight into a pub and up to the bar, and stay there all night; but not you. You'll carefully select some little corner to occupy, quite near the back, but within sight of the door. Pisceans, another Water sign, always sit near the door, or in sight of it, in case they need to escape, but you simply want to watch it. The idea behind this is that you won't be on view to someone as soon as they walk it, but you'll be able to see them. There's one other thing, too: you always sit near the toilets. Sounds funny, but it's true; and it's not because you need to use them more than the other signs, either.

There are such things as pub names which are associated with the sign, and you might like to try some of them. Scorpionic names are those which include any liquor container, or the number eight; for example, The Flask, the Three Barrels, The Eight Bells. Also yours is any pub called the Turk's Head, and any pub with smuggling associations.

When it comes to drinks, you are going to choose something which is strong, dark, and concentrated. Most lager is too light for you — both in flavour and in colour — so you might find yourself ordering Guinness. Older Scorpios enjoy spirits, which have the strength and concentration they want. Female Scorpios' taste falls somewhere in between, and you will often choose aperitifs or spirits with mixers; again, the drink has to be strong, and dark in colour, often red.

Sports and pastimes

Despite being ruled by Mars, Scorpios aren't tremendous athletes, and you're nowhere near as active a player as Mars' other sign, the Arians.

You do have a lot of physical energy, and it needs exercising, but you also have a great deal of mental energy, and you exercise that by concentration. Sports which appeal to you are those which require concentration and control, and which also entail a fair degree of risk.

Two sports which are particularly Scorpionic are underwater swimming, which has already been mentioned, and pot-holing. The tighter the space in which you have to work, and the greater the risk, the more you like it. Putting the two together, as in the extremely risky activity of cave diving, is probably the ultimate Scorpio experience.

Motorized sports are something else that you like. Motorcycling has a particular appeal; its combination of power and speed balanced against danger, controlled by intense concentration, is very much your sort of thing.

Pastimes, which suggest by their very name that they are pursued at a more relaxed pace, are something you are usually too busy to spend time on. Since concentration and getting your own way (in the best possible sense) satisfy you, you are quite happy to work long hours, and fill your spare time with extra work. A Scorpio needs to be constantly testing himself to the limit, stretching the boundaries to bursting point, and sometimes beyond. If a sport or pastime doesn't offer that sort of experience, then it has no attraction for you.

Colour and style

Scorpio style in clothes is unmistakable. It is much admired, often imitated, and very direct. The whole purpose of it is to produce a reaction in the onlooker, and to make the wearer appear powerful. You're trying to communicate that intensity of power and concentration that you have, and also how much you have it under control; at the same time, you're trying to provoke a strong emotion in everyone you meet, because then you know where you are with them.

To do this you go for styles which give a solid and compact outline, suggesting the concentrated energy within, you only move when it's absolutely necessary, so it isn't important for you to have clothes which allow freedom of movement. In particular, if a certain item requires you to be in motion for it to be seen at its best, then you will decide that it's not your style. Clothes with extra pleats or folds, or anything which hangs heavily until you animate it with your own movements, are not your style either.

Neither is anything with a great deal of decoration, or which might be described as 'frilly' or 'pretty'; such things suggest a light and outgoing personality, unlikely to take things seriously, and you have a more strongly defined character than that. Short, straight lines, and sharp angles, forming 'V' shapes, are better suited to you.

Your reputation for dressing sexily comes about for two reasons. The first is the colours that you choose, which are red and black, the colours of the sign, but also the colours of passion and death, and so charged with a special emotional intensity. The effect would be very different if you were to dress in a pale green, for example, but for a Scorpio that's not very likely.

The second reason is that you like your clothes to be tight, and even to restrict your movements a little. This is to do with *containing* the powerful energies within you, but at the same time it gives an indication of just how strong those inner forces are, and displays your body against the fabric, too. Your liking for tight clothes and dramatic colours is maintained even when fashion dictates otherwise: you know what you like and you stay with it. One of the reasons that Scorpionic style is so recognizable is that it doesn't change much over the years: it is always tight, dramatic, concentrated.

Tight leather is something usually associated with Scorpio, and it's not hard to see why. The strength of the material, the associations it has with protection and power, and the sensual response produced in the wearer by its feel and smell are all very Scorpionic, despite the fact that the material itself is actually associated with another sign, Capricorn. Any association with tightness is strictly Scorpionic: Capricorns like to wear their clothes a little looser.

Scorpio women enjoy wearing, and suit, high heels, for the usual Scorpio reasons. They restrict movement, they display the foot, and they produce a reaction. This is also the sign which is said to enjoy wearing boots most, and you may well have more boots than shoes: check and see.

In general, you look good in business clothes, like suits, and rather less good in sportswear. The reasons for this are that sportswear is usually looser in cut and lighter in colour, and both of these prevent you from showing the intensity of your personality properly.

Work

Two words sum up the Scorpio career plan: *hidden power*. They don't have to be taken together, though of course they can be, but whatever you choose to do, it is more than likely that it will either be hidden in some way, as in out of the public eye, or that it will involve you controlling things, either processes or people.

The hidden jobs are the ones which attract you. There is a strong attraction for Scorpios in police work, especially criminal investigation. The idea of finding things which are hidden, delving into secrets, is very close to your heart, as is the controlling authority which comes with being a police officer. For the same reasons, and even more hidden from the public view, it is said that Scorpios make excellent espionage agents.

The sign is also connected with the removal of things which are no longer required, and so demolition, sanitation, and waste disposal are businesses which attract Scorpios. Undertaking and funeral arrangement is Scorpionic, too.

The careers which have more to do with power than this being hidden are many, but more often than not you will want to concern yourself with *financial* power, and Scorpios often do very well in financial services, banking, and insurance. They do well as tax inspectors, too! The aim, as far as you are concerned, is to be in control, but not necessarily to be 'up front' or on view in any way.

Your career progress is usually excellent — that concentration of energy you bring to everything else you do will make sure that you get to where you want to be in the shortest possible time. You are also very, very good at internal politics — that process whereby you find out who knows who and who is likely to be promoted, so that you can manoeuvre things behind the scenes. No other sign except Capricorn has your talent for getting to the top of a large organization — and you needn't fear each other, because he gets there by sheer hard work, while you take a less obvious route.

To sum up, things to go for:
- Any job where the real power is behind the scenes;
- Anything concerned with finance;
- Anything 'dark' or little known.

Things to avoid:
- Jobs where you meet or serve the public;
- Anything where you actually make the product yourself;
- Anything which is constantly changing.

People

You like people who are:
- determined;
- passionate;
- successful.

You dislike people who:
- seem aloof, superior;
- blame circumstances rather than themselves;
- have no strong opinions or desires.

SAGITTARIUS

Home

Your home is probably a wonderful mess, full of muddy boots, things from foreign lands, and lots and lots of books. Your casual, rather untidy personal style transfers itself to your home quite easily, but the good thing about it is that nobody ever feels that they have to behave in a certain way when they come to visit. It's a place for people to be at ease in, and everyone feels comfortable the moment they arrive.

Your furniture is likely to be rather large, and quite hefty, because it has to withstand you throwing yourself around on it, and generally abusing it. Warm autumnal colours predominate, such as reds and browns; white and blue are too cool for your taste. You are far more likely to spend time in the kitchen than in a sitting room or bedroom; it's the most informal place in any house, and it's where you can do something about the immense appetite you bring home with you each time you return.

There will always be books, in every room, along with newspapers and magazines — kept because they have something in them which has excited your interest — and of course maps, which all Sagittarians love, because they remind you of travelling.

Cars

Sagittarians get a great deal of pleasure out of cars. You have the love of machinery and speed that your Fire sign colleagues the Arians have, and a love of travelling which is all your own; together they explain the way you feel about your car.

What you like best about your car is driving it. That may sound obvious, but the fact is that most of the other signs buy their cars for reasons other than the pleasure of driving them; only the Fire signs — Aries, Leo, and you, Sagittarius — put the experience of driving at the top of the list of things a car has to offer. And even the Leo would sometimes rather be chauffeured, so that just leaves you and the Arian.

What the Earth signs want, for example, is for the car to be comfortable, a sort of living room on wheels, where the smell of the leather seats and the whirr of the electric windows is more rewarding than actually driving it. Ask your Taurean or Capricornian friends (if you have any — see the diagram on page 194) about their cars, and you'll soon see that the depth of the paint means more to them than the sound of the engine.

Water signs want security and anonymity; they see their car as a suit of armour which keeps them safe from the outside world. It's hard to imagine that as a principal consideration when buying a car, isn't it?

You see, you're such a purist. You don't need protecting, because you're so open and so optimistic. You don't need cosseting with material comforts either, because you'd rather be actively involved than sit still. You see the car in its purest sense, as a machine for travelling in.

The difference between you and the Arian is that he sees a car as a travelling *machine*, and you see it as a *travelling* machine. What matters most to him is the roar of the exhaust and how fast it goes, and though you like these too, your interest lies in how far it will take you.

The idea of distance is the key to understanding

Sagittarian thought, and to your love of cars. Some people use cars for convenience, for going down to the shops, but long-legged Sagittarians can walk there just as quickly; what you buy your car for is to go adventuring, not shopping.

It doesn't really matter whether you regularly drive to Rome, or Vienna, or not; the essential thing is that you'd like to think that you could, and the idea of doing it has a tremendous appeal to you. You choose your car to represent the idea of going long distances, and to show that you are a person who loves travelling.

For these reasons you are unlikely to choose a small car, or a short one, given the choice. A small car may be all that you can afford at the moment, or maybe your car comes with your job, but if you were given the choice, your eye would be drawn to something rather longer or larger than the average family hatchback. Size is an important consideration: people with big ideas and big personalities choose big cars, and a Sagittarian's ideas are bigger than almost anybody else's. Similarly, Sagittarians are usually tall, and long in the leg, which all ties in with the idea of travelling long distances, of course, and so you choose a car which is long in the leg too; the long and elegant lines of a Jaguar, say, are much more appealing to you than, for example, the rather rounder outline of a family car.

All the virtues of a small car, such as its nippiness, economy, and the lightness of its controls, are lost on you, because your imagination always see the far horizon as the goal rather than practical details. What you eventually buy is probably far too large and cumbersome for dense city traffic, and rather tiring to drive, but if it has any of the romance of motoring attached to it then you're happy. Old sports cars are a common Sagittarian purchase, because the sensation of actually travelling is usually stronger in them than in a quiet and well-insulated modern saloon.

Sagittarius has long been associated with horses.

This may be the reason why some Sagittarians are attracted to cars which can be called 'thoroughbreds', in that they come from long-established names with a glorious past. MG, Riley, Alfa Romeo: these are Sagittarian cars, full of the romance of motoring, and far more attractive to you than the cold but efficient technology of today. You like their shapes — the curves of twenty years ago appeal more to Jupiter's sign than straight lines — and you like their colours, too: rich reds and maroons are more to Sagittarian taste than the silvers and greys which predominate today.

One car which associates itself with horses is the Range Rover, and it makes a perfect car for a Sagittarian, too. It is as tall as you are, giving you a higher and better view (*very* Sagittarian), and it can go anywhere, which is exactly what you want to do. The idea of being able to travel to the ends of the earth, over high mountains and across deserts, is one which constantly fascinates you, and cars which promise this, like Range Rovers and Jeeps, are something you would dearly love to own. As with the long-legged European touring car or the classic thoroughbred sports car, the practicalities of owning such things should really put you off buying one, but you always ignore little details like that. It is the ideal of travel, and the sensation of going places, which exert the strongest pull.

Food
Food to you is fuel, something that you need to keep up your active lifestyle. You enjoy it, and you like eating it, but it has to be said that you would probably enjoy it more if you ate it rather more slowly; Sagittarians wolf down their food.

There are some signs, notably Taurus, who make food into something close to a religion, and there are other signs, like Gemini, who hardly eat at all, and take little interest in what is set before them. You fall somewhere between the two.

Like the other two Fire signs, Aries and Leo, your appetite could be described as 'hearty'; you enjoy substantial meals whose main ingredient is meat. All the Fire signs like eating meat — Aries the most, it is said — but the Sagittarian speciality is game, both furred and feathered. It may be that the rich and strong flavours appeal to you, or it may be that the sign of the Archer feels that proper meat has to be hunted before it can be brought to the table; whichever it is, if the menu has pheasant or venison to offer, they'll be the ones you'll choose.

Nor is it hard to understand your liking for Indian and Chinese food. Anything which comes from far away, evoking that idea of distant places and long journeys, has a special appeal for you. So, too, does American food, the sort of food you can eat while you are on the move. Once again, it isn't the flavour, it's the idea of travel.

You are attracted by food which is rich or spicy in flavour, and which is a dark red in colour. Food which is pale, or whose predominant colour is green, seems less attractive to you. Red vegetables, like tomatoes, are fine — it's all to do with the colour.

Your favourite dish is probably something like goulash, which manages to combine most of the things that you like as far as colour, flavour and content goes. It also has the advantages of being foreign in origin, and being easy to eat, because it is an unfortunate fact that although Sagittarians have many talents, finesse at the table isn't one of them.

Holidays

You love going on holiday. You're addicted to the process of travelling. Even the things that everybody else hates, such as waiting at the airport, or the flight itself, are fun for you. And since the travelling itself is so enjoyable, it doesn't really matter about the destination. Every destination is full of fascination for you, and the harder it is to get there, the better you like it.

It is quite possible that you would like to spend your entire holiday travelling; the idea of a plane ticket which enables you to cover the whole continental network served by a particular airline, or a round-the-world ticket, must appeal to you. So must the idea of a railpass, or of crossing Asia on the Trans-Siberian railway.

When you eventually get to where you're going, you don't head for the beach like everyone else, you explore the surrounding area. Sitting still isn't a rest for a Sagittarian, it's an illness; being active, mobile, inquisitive, finding things out, is what refreshes and restores you.

The places you would most like to visit are those which are part of the romantic traveller's tales of old: China, via the silk road, or India via the spice-trading routes. What you want is to feel that you have really travelled, and that the places you visit are very different from what you are used to. There's nothing worse, for you, than to go to some resort where every effort has been made to make things similar to the way they are at home.

For hundreds of years now, various countries of the world have been associated with the signs of the zodiac. Perhaps you might like to try visiting a few Sagittarian places. In Europe they include the whole of mainland Spain, the Tuscany region of Italy, and the Dalmatian coast of Yugoslavia. Further afield there's Arabia, and for those determined to go somewhere different, the island of Madagascar.

Drinks

Sagittarius is a very social sign, and you usually enjoy visiting your local pub. Some signs go to pubs to drink, and some for company, but what Sagittarians do is get into long and involved philosophical discussions which last deep into the night. Philosophy and alcohol are both connected, astrologically, to Jupiter, so it's not surprising that Jupiter's sign has its best thoughts in the bar.

Like the other Fire signs, you stand or sit in plain view, unlike the Water signs, who hide in the corners, but you always make sure that you are in sight of the door. This isn't because you might need to escape, but so that you are the first to see if anyone new and interesting should walk in.

As always, you are attracted to things which come from far away. The local ale may be excellent, but if there is an imported beer from somewhere interesting like Czechoslovakia, then you'll have that, and spend the evening looking at the label on the bottle, imagining what the town must look like where it was brewed.

Sports and pastimes

Sagittarians, along with Arians, are the great sportsmen of the zodiac. The difference between you is that Arians are individual performers, often choosing something like athletics, whereas Sagittarians are team members, preferring to play in company. You are also more likely to play games for their own sake; you like to win, of course, but you don't mind losing as long as you've had a good game. The English idea of sporting fair play is a very Sagittarian one.

The sign is supposed to have a liking for all equestrian sports. This is true, but it also has a liking for all motorized sports, and for all sports where the player gets muddy; cross-country running and rugby football are prime examples.

Riding and hunting are very close to the heart of the sign. All Sagittarian sports have a boisterous good humour to them, and are rather dirty, being connected to the countryside or to the farmyard in one sense or another. You have a natural scruffiness, an inability to stay clean, which doesn't matter at all when you're around dogs or horses, but which is part of the reasons

why Sagittarians aren't usually attracted to tennis: the
neatness and cleanness of the game and its costume
are very un-Sagittarian.

Away from the playing field, Sagittarians play with
travelling machines of all kinds, such as cars or old
aeroplanes, and in the evenings you read. There is no
subject which has no interest for you — you will read
anything and everything, and to the disgust of the other
eleven signs, you can remember most of it afterwards.
Nothing is ever wasted on you: there is always
something which is of value to you, and which you will
be glad to know at some time in the future.

Colour and style

Sagittarians are not the zodiac's snappiest dressers. No
matter how hard you try, you always look rather out of
place in formal clothes, and you find them extremely
uncomfortable; they make you feel stiff and unnatural,
and you hate it.

What you need from your clothes is freedom of
movement, and the ability to travel well. Formal clothes
encourage you to stay still, and the pockets are usually
too small to put anything useful in. Useful to a Sagittarian,
that is, such as half a dozen books that you happen to be
reading, or an interesting thing from a junkshop which
you happened to buy on your way home.

You are at your best in soft, warm clothes, which suit
your friendly and outdoor lifestyle. Most of the time you
are happy in jeans and a sweater, and indeed some of
you are quite likely to wear this combination to events
and occasions with fairly strict dress codes, as if such
things didn't apply to you. You reason that if you are
going to be at your best, and enjoy yourself, then you
have to be comfortable; if you feel strangled by your
collar then you are unlikely to want to stay for long.

Every so often you decide that you need some more
clothes, and go on a spending spree. What's unusual
about this is that you have a tendency to buy rather

flashy, expensive stuff (extravagance is one of Jupiter's qualities) which is probably unsuited to your lifestyle. It all becomes rather battered and well-worn in a few weeks anyway, because your rough-and-tumble life makes such demands on it.

Your favourite, and most useful, item of clothing is probably your jacket, and you are likely to have lots of them, probably in outdoor styles, such as waxed cotton shooting jackets, or down-filled ski jackets. The reason that you wear these rather than coats is that they don't hamper your legs, something which annoys you, and because they have lots of useful pockets.

You also like anything which is connected to the idea of travelling, such as flying jackets, or anything which suggests wide open spaces, such as Western styles. Motorcycle jackets are a favourite, too.

The preferred Sagittarian colour is always blue — preferably a deep shade, almost navy. You choose big motifs to match your big ideas, rather than fussy little prints, but most of the time you go for plain colours; they give a relaxed impression, and that's the most important thing about the Sagittarian style. It may not be chic, and it certainly isn't neat, but it's relaxed.

Work

At work, you need to be involved in the transmission of ideas, and preferably to be mobile as well, if you are to feel at all satisfied. If your job has no opportunity for you to show what you can do and what you know, then it isn't for you. There is nothing which you cannot understand once you put your mind to it — Sagittarians are blessed with the finest mind in the zodiac — but there is a real risk that it will be under-used, and so you become bored.

What you must be particularly careful to avoid is anything which involves repetition, especially if the work itself is intricate or detailed, such as inspecting things for errors, or assembling small parts: in these circumstances your mind will refuse to operate properly, and you will make lots of mistakes. You need to be involved in bigger things, basically.

Lots of Sagittarians are teachers, which suits your abilities very well. It's a lively, talkative sort of job, but it's also one where you get a chance to give other people the benefit of your knowledge, which is something that gives you great satisfaction of the kind which is so deep that you can't easily describe it to someone who doesn't know the feeling for themselves. The same applies to medicine, which is another Sagittarian profession: it's to do with applying your knowledge for the benefit of others.

Knowledge is something you Sagittarians value highly, and a career either publishing or selling books will appeal. So will anything connected with languages, such as translating, or perhaps dealing with books and magazines in foreign languages.

Two old and respectable professions which have always been connected to the sign are the legal profession in all its various forms, and the Church. As always with Sagittarius, the business of both of these lies with ideas rather than objects.

Some Sagittarians prefer their work to be out of doors and to keep them mobile. The transportation and haulage trades are full of Sagittarians at all levels who prefer to be on the move than to be behind a desk all day, even if their career development becomes limited. Freedom always outweighs money to this sign.

Finally, animals, and specifically horses, always have a place in your affections. Sagittarians can be found racing, breeding and riding horses; as vets; and as bookies, tipsters, and gamblers, too. Wherever there are horses, there are Sagittarians.

To sum up, things to go for:
- Any job which gives you a chance to use what you know;

- Any job which is changeable and has no set routine;
- Any job which involves travel.

Things to avoid:
- Fine detail work;
- Jobs where strict rules are kept to and independence is frowned on;
- Jobs where the end product is an object rather than an idea.

People

You like people who are:
- outgoing;
- optimistic;
- open and forthright.

You dislike people who:
- take life too seriously;
- have no belief in providence;
- deliberately mislead or take advantage of others.

CAPRICORN

Home

A Capricorn home is likely to be an impressive place. Not necessarily comfortable, but very impressive. Everything in it will be of the finest quality available; visitors will find themselves thinking not so much about the colour or the style, but about the cost.

Some Capricorns have rather a plain taste in furnishing, where the carpets are of a neutral colour, and there is almost no decoration at all. Chairs tend to be hard and upright rather than low and softly cushioned, and the whole place can feel rather severe, as though softness was weakness in some way.

Other Capricorns prefer a traditional look to their homes, with heavy furniture and deep carpets in rich colours. There is usually an emphasis on dark wood, and the style is often taken from a period in history, such as Jacobean or Regency rather than modern; it is the Capricorn feeling for tradition and history coming out.

Whatever the style, Capricorn homes have a sort of orderliness that some of the other signs find disturbing. They are there not so much as a private retreat at the end of the day, but as a public exhibition of a lifestyle. They are there to be lived in, to be sure, but they are also there to be seen, and possibly envied, by others as well.

Cars

Cars are important to a Capricorn; more important, perhaps, than to any other sign. Nowadays, a car is more than a machine to get you around the place or take you on your holidays — it's a mobile statement of who you are and what position you occupy. In other words, it's a status symbol.

Status symbols are something which Capricorns understand, almost without thinking about it. This is the sign whose natural instinct is to climb to the top, and to tell the world about it. There are some signs who feel that they were *born* superior — like Leos, for instance — and there are some who feel that they have to work hard to get there. Capricorns fall into this category. You feel that you have worked hard for your rewards, and you want to be able to show the world what it is that you've worked for. The easiest way to do that is with objects of wealth and status, like big cars and big houses.

The Fire signs, like Aries and Sagittarius, are interested in a car for its performance, for the feeling of travelling at speed. You're slightly different. Performance is important, but what you're really interested in is the quality of the machine itself, the luxury features, and above all the position it occupies in everyone else's view of things.

No matter how brilliantly it performed, you could never be persuaded to buy a car which was small, cheap, or less than lavishly equipped. It might be very cheap to run, but that doesn't matter to you, and no amount of fun to be had driving the thing will compensate you for the fact that it is seen as rather basic transport. This is why Capricorns tend not to buy little runabouts.

Whichever car takes your eye, or whichever one fits your budget, you will always find yourself looking at the version with the bigger engine, or the higher level of trim, or the exclusive paintwork. What you want is for people to see you as being that little bit higher up than the normal. Some people (Aquarians, probably) would call this showing off, but you yourself would call it justifiable *pride* in your own achievements.

The Earth signs, which is the group of three zodiac signs to which you belong (the others are Virgo and Taurus), all appreciate the physical qualities of a car. The fit of the components, the smell of the seats, and the thickness of the carpets all matter more to you than how well it goes round corners. Taureans are the ones who care most about comfort, while the Virgos bother about loose nuts and bolts, or bits of trim that have come undone; what matters most to you is that the whole thing should feel firm and well-built, and that the paintwork has a deep shine.

You want your car to remind you, every time you get in it, of how fine a person you are, and of how well you deserve a car as fine as it is. To you, it is an expression of your career so far. If you are a superior person, then it must be a superior car. If you are hard but capable, then it must be so too; and if you are an upholder of traditional values, then it must somehow show those as well.

You are a great believer in the hierarchy of things: beneath the director are the managers, and assistants. Young secretaries and trainees have hatchbacks, for example, while managers have something larger, and senior managers or directors have limousines. Once you have gone up a rung of the ladder yourself, you would *never* have a car which represented a lower position — though you might have one representing a higher position if you were very ambitious, just to show where you expected yourself to be going.

So, which car would you choose, if money were no object? The answer is quite simple: BMW. Their cars represent the Capricorn way of thinking more exactly than any other, and for this reason they are sought after by anyone who wants to be seen as a success — anyone who wants to show Capricorn values, in fact.

The similarity between these cars and the Capricorn view of life is visible in all sorts of ways. To begin with, they are expensive, and that assumes a certain level of success if you are to be able to afford one. They also come in Capricorn's colours — grey and black — to give an image of seriousness and authority. They have tradition and history, important to Capricorns, and they have that well-built feel that is so reassuring to all the Earth signs. Finally, they have extremely fine paintwork, an almost impenetrable exterior polish which has a peculiar appeal to the Capricorn kind.

It is of course quite possible that you may choose another car, but whatever it is it will still be large, well-built, dark in colour, expensive, from the top end of its range or class, and the paintwork will gleam.

Food

Compared to the high importance Capricorns attach to their cars, you pay relatively little attention to your food. This is surprising, since your other Earth sign colleagues are both very particular about what they eat. Taureans, in particular, are addicted to food, they give it the same importance that you give to money and a successful career. Virgoans are very careful about the quality of the food they eat, and are often vegetarian, but not you. Often you will go without food if you are too busy to take a break, and when you do eat, you will make do with something simple. Like the mountain goat which is part of the animal of the sign, you can get by on virtually nothing, if you have to.

There is a certain sort of Capricorn who allows himself so little in the way of creature comforts that he risks his health by eating so little and so poorly, but even for the vast majority of you who take better care of yourselves, the idea of indulging yourself through eating seems odd.

What you prefer to eat is something that you have met before, and which is simple. You're not as adventurous in your tastes as the Aquarian, nor as fond of rich flavours as the Scorpio: good old meat and vegetables in the traditional manner is more your sort of thing. Once a dish becomes *established*, so that everyone eats it and it isn't considered unusual any more then it becomes part of your diet too, but while it's considered a bit daring, you won't try it.

Elaborate food, which has had much time spent on it, and which is accompanied by rich sauces, is not to your taste. It might be argued that since such dishes are the most expensive on the menu, you might be drawn to them in the same way that you are attracted to expensive cars, but that isn't so: you have a liking for food plain and simple, so that you can taste the quality of the ingredients, and virtually see them on the plate in front of you. That's the Earth-sign influence at work. You never forget that food is fuel; other people may see it as a pastime, as art, or as a sensual experience, but not you.

Holidays

A Capricorn's idea of a good holiday contains two things: history, and hard ground.

Not everybody actually likes sitting under a hot sun

for two weeks doing nothing. You Capricorns don't usually like the sun much at all, which isn't surprising since you were born in the depths of winter. Also, because you work so hard, and are used to it, the idea of doing nothing seems funny to you; you need to be working away, struggling onwards and upwards, before you feel that you are properly occupied.

That's where the hard ground comes in. Capricorns are goats, to some extent, and goats live high in the hills, where the ground is hard and the grass is sparse. Wherever the ground is hard and uneven beneath your feet, then you are happy. Lots of Capricorns love walking over hills, and those who are really keen go climbing mountains, too. Outdoor holidays appeal very strongly to you, and even if you haven't got time for more than a few days away, then a weekend walking in the fells will do you more good than a weekend in some beach resort. Even when you do fly to the sun, you will notice, perhaps, that you leave your companions on the beach and go for a walk. Perhaps you've never thought about it before, but the chances are that you have gone for a scramble up to a headland, or a walk along a cliff path, or something like that, never into the town or down to the market. Always it is the high ground and the hard path that attract you.

History, the other ingredient of the Capricorn holiday, appeals to you because more than any other sign you have a feeling for tradition and the passing of time. If there are old ruins or a cathedral to see, then you're sure to pay it a visit. The solidness of the stonework and the efforts of the people who built it have a real meaning for you. Best of all, of course, is a holiday where you can combine the two elements, as in climbing over ruins, or walking to a remote high fortress.

Centuries ago the countries of the world were given their own zodiac signs, and you might find that a country which shares your sign provides an enjoyable spot for a holiday. Mainland Greece and Yugoslavia are Capricornian, as well as parts of the Alps — all of them places with plenty of hard, high ground for you to walk on.

Drinks

Capricorns aren't great drinkers, on the whole. *Dry* is a good word to describe Capricorns generally, and that doesn't match the idea of great quantities of liquid. Not that you're averse to alcohol, just that you don't like a lot of liquid. You like things that are dry in flavour, too, as opposed to sweet, so brown ale, which is both sweet and wet, is generally not your choice.

What you tend to go for are spirits, which are strong without having volume, and which are usually dry in flavour. It is quite possible that whisky may be your favourite, but it's more suited to a Leo than a Capricorn; you're more likely to choose gin. And, since you're always conservative when it comes to recipes, that means gin and tonic rather than anything too adventurous or too modern.

You're quite happy to be noticed when you're in a pub, and in fact you rather enjoy it, so you stand in the middle. That may sound obvious, but next time you're out, notice how the Scorpios hide in the corners at the back, and how the Pisceans are always near the door; the only people in the centre are you and the Leos. The difference between you is that the Leos like to draw attention to themselves whereas you don't, but that's not the same thing as not wanting to be noticed; you like to be seen, but not to be too loud about it. Noticeable but not obvious, that's your motto.

Sports and pastimes

Capricorns don't have a lot of time for sports, or so it is usually said. You do spend a lot of time working, it is true, and your career means more to you than any other part of your life, but that doesn't mean that you never do anything for your own amusement.

Games as such, that is things played for the fun of it, are a difficult thing for you to understand, however. You are very serious in your outlook on life, and very hard on yourself in your approach to it. It's all very well for the other signs to play games for fun, and to shrug their shoulders when they lose, but you play games to win, and to win only; losing is something that really hurts, because it means that somebody else is better than you, and that puts you *down* the ladder a rung or two.

Perhaps because you find it difficult to play games for fun, you tend to play games on your own, and away from other people. In any case, what you're really interested in is getting better at whatever the sport demands; the social side of things, in that you have team-mates or fellow players, doesn't hold much attraction for you. The exception to this is when you join a sports club as a stepping-stone in your career, so that you are seen by important people who also play tennis, or golf, or whatever.

What you prefer are games for one player, where toughness and endurance are required. Sports needing muscle don't attract you — Capricorns aren't usually very muscular anyway — but those which call for long and sustained efforts have a strong appeal. Typical Capricorn sports include rock-climbing, long-distance cycling, and marathon running, all of which require a lean, hard sort of fitness, which is very Capricornian. These activities have become very popular just lately, which has something to do with the influence of the outer planets, which affect all of us, and which are currently in Capricorn.

When not out running or climbing, Capricorns enjoy quiet but constructive pastimes like improving their homes or their gardens. Always, the idea is to do something which improves on what went before, and which will last. When forced to stay indoors, you read history and biography; the struggles, and the successes, of those who have made it to the top before you are more satisfying to you than any piece of fiction.

Colour and style

Capricorn colours have one thing in common — they are dark. The real colour of the sign, if it can be called that, is black, but dark greys are also associated with it, and so are sombre browns and deep greens. Bright colours are not for you.

The use of dark colours always gives an aura of power and authority to whatever you wear, and you carefully combine this with clean, simple shapes and lines to maintain the impression of status and prestige without going over the top into the dramatic, which is what Scorpios do when they use dark colours.

Capricorn style is always traditional, conservative, and expensive. Business suits, for both sexes, are a Capricorn fashion, and their neat lines, absence of decoration, and dark colours are all hallmarks of the sign. Simple quality is what counts in a Capricorn style, and even when everyone else is dressing in the same way, as is the case in the late 1980's (the outer planets in Capricorn are the reason), then the true Capricorn still manages to find cloth of a higher quality, a deeper colour, a cleaner and more elegant cut.

Capricorn fashion encloses things, and hides the body from view. Collars and scarves hide the neck, while hats and gloves hide the head and hands. Other signs can't be bothered with gloves, but Capricorns feel incomplete without them. Similarly, Capricorn shoes are elegant, superior, and traditional. They are also extremely highly polished, as Capricorn cars are. For women, high heels are preferred; they add height, and thus status and superiority.

Weight of clothing becomes important, because light

clothes don't have the same feeling of power and status to them. You always prefer an overcoat to an outdoor jacket, and you never mind the weight of a garment as long as it is of the finest quality.

Work

The real home of the Capricorn is the large organization. Better than anyone else, you understand the way such things run. There are levels of command, and people who are responsible for this but not for that, and above all there is a feeling of security: the company looks after everybody, and it has a firm framework of rules to help it function. All of this makes perfect sense to you, and you love it. You instinctively know who is important and who isn't, and you always use the rules to your own advantage, rather than strangling yourself with them as the Sagittarians and the Aquarians do. The person who goes all the way up the ladder from tea-boy to Managing Director is the Capricorn, every time.

The larger the organization, the better you like it. Working for yourself, with the freedom to decide what you do and when, is never a good idea for someone like you, so don't try it unless you're very sure of what you're doing. You're much better off climbing the ranks of a large company.

You're better off, too, working with money rather than people. Face-to-face confrontations aren't really your forte — to begin with, you're not a fluent talker, and you tend to keep yourself to yourself, and besides that, you feel far more at home with hard facts and figures than you do with moods and emotions.

Your natural position, of course, is at the top, and in due course you will get there — Capricorns always do. You are particularly well suited for the job, in fact; you take a serious attitude to your responsibilities, you always have a regard for tradition and what has gone before, you don't make a move until you are sure about it, and you drive yourself at least as hard as anyone else, if not harder. You are the perfect senior management candidate. In fact, if your current job gives you no opportunity to take responsibility for something, no matter how small, and offers you no chance of promotion, then you are in the wrong job.

Apart from finance, in all its branches from banks to insurance, the preferred fields for Capricorns to work in are large companies which deal with solid and long-lasting products, such as the construction industry. Buildings of all kinds are very Capricornian. Property development and estate agency are also suitable, except for the actual selling; that's best left to a Gemini.

Finally, there is a connection between the sign of Capricorn and your bones and teeth, there are lots of Capricorn dentists, too.

To sum up, things to go for:
- Any job involving money or numeric data
- Any job with a well-defined career plan in a large company
- Any of the 'professions': doctor, lawyer . . .

Things to avoid:
- Working on your own initiative;
- Work where person-to-person contact is important;
- Work which changes quickly or has no set pattern.

People
You like people who are:
- Ambitious;
- Fair-minded;
- Responsible.

You dislike people who:
- Ignore the rules and take short cuts;
- Say anything that comes into their heads;
- Let their emotions rule their actions.

Aquarius

Home

Aquarian homes have a definite feel to them. They seem to have been designed for people to slow down, spread out, and have time to think; what they most definitely don't do is overwhelm the visitor with sensations and impressions.

The cosy and traditional look, with large pieces of furniture, heavily patterned carpets, and everything gathered around the hearth, is hard to find in an Aquarian house. Instead, the predominant colours are greys and blues and most of the furniture is rather low, so that the rooms seem taller and more spread out than is actually the case; the emphasis is on the horizontal rather than the vertical, and this helps people feel relaxed.

The furniture itself is likely to be rather modern, and often in the metal-and-glass style; glass is something which is particularly suited to, and chosen by, Aquarians. Even if the furniture is made of more traditional wood and fabric, the Aquarian's choice is for lighter, slimmer styles rather than anything heavy, bulky, or oppressively dark.

There is a cool feeling to Aquarian homes which is nothing to do with the temperature; it is to do with the neutral colours, and the simple furnishing. Furniture is cleverly arranged so that a group of people feel close enough to be friendly, but not forced to be with each other; it is that distinctive Aquarian blend of friendliness and independence, as always.

Cars

Cars are an essential part of the Aquarian lifestyle, and yet oddly enough this is one of the signs *least* likely to own one, or to look longingly at the latest models.

What you actually want a car to do is to take you from one place to another, and in particular to take you to see your friends and to help you enjoy a fuller and wider social life. The business of *communication* — where people are brought into contact with each other — is one of the most important things in your life.

It may seem obvious to you that a car should be used this way, but it is by no means so obvious to the other signs, for example, the Earth signs (Taurus, Virgo, and Capricorn) see a car as primarily a status symbol, something they own which they can touch and feel, and be reassured by; things such as the gleam of the paintwork and the depth of the carpets are very important to these signs, yet not to you. Perhaps you have wondered who the advertisements were aimed at, the ones with the beautifully photographed cars in front of the large country houses. Now you know.

There are also some people who use their cars as a sort of retreat, a little fortress on wheels where they can feel safe from the world outside. Cancerians, Scorpios, and Pisceans are like this. You're not, though: you positively enjoy meeting other people, and indeed one of the reasons that you have a car in the first place is so that you can meet *more* people.

You are sure enough about yourself and your opinions (that Aquarian logic again) not to need your car to convince you that you are somebody special, or to protect you from the world outside. This means that your car doesn't have to be particularly new, or luxurious; nor does it have to go unnoticed and hide in the crowd. In fact, the opposite is true: you like to celebrate your independence, and so you quite enjoy owning the sort of car that nobody else would think of buying, and you like to be among friends, so you are likely to buy a car with room to take your friends as well as yourself.

The most important element in all this is the social impulse; that means that the actual process of driving the car is a secondary consideration, and probably isn't much of a consideration. Some signs get really rather

worked up about the actual sensation of driving —
Aries and Sagittarius usually — but that kind of passion
for speed isn't part of the Aquarian character, so if you
have a bright red sports car, it's to show that you are
different from everybody else rather than because you
have a deep passion for driving it. The only exceptions
to this are if it is mechanically temperamental, or if it is a
convertible, for reasons I'll explain later on.

Since all you ask of a car is that it runs and takes you
where you want to go, the choice is very wide. Virtually
anything will do, and frequently does, but there are one
or two Aquarian favourites which seem to have a
special attraction for you.

The first of these is a van or minibus of some kind.
Perhaps it is because they have room for all your
friends as well as yourself. Aquarians who work for
good causes always seem to have a minibus or a
camper van, usually proudly displaying a number of
stickers proclaiming half a dozen good causes, often
ecological ones.

The second Aquarian favourite is the French car. Part
of the reason for this is that they are, or were, relatively
unusual, and this appealed to the Aquarian need to
stand out in the crowd. Another part of it is that until a
few years ago when they became more standardized,
French cars had a few mechanical quirks all their own,
which were quite logical once understood, but none
the less odd — and therefore exactly the sort of thing a
logical but nonconformist person like an Aquarian
would love. Almost anything produced by Citroën is
ideal for an Aquarian.

Many Aquarians take a particular delight in
mechanical quirkiness. There is something about
machinery, perhaps its combination of logic and
ingenuity, which appeals to Aquarian men, in
particular; they find it much more rewarding to get to
know an engine than to get to know a person. This is
the 'technical' or 'scientific' side of the Aquarian in

action, and it is easy to see in his choice of car. An old car, which may well need more mechanical sympathy than most, is likely to receive far more love and devotion from an Aquarian than his girlfriend does.

Finally, it has to be remembered that Aquarius is an Air sign, along with Gemini and Libra, and that means that you like to feel yourself in your element — with the wind on your face. Open-air motoring always has a special appeal for you, so an old convertible for sale will always be something to make you stop and look. One day you'll buy one, you know you will.

Aquarians seem to have taken to the age of the computer better than the rest of the signs, and a car which presents a high-tech appearance, and which has many computerized features, may have a strong appeal.

Food

Aquarius as a sign is ruled by the planet Saturn, just as your neighbouring sign Capricorn is, and one of the things that signs associated with Saturn have in common is the low importance they place on food. To be a real glutton — or a real gourmet — it's best if you're from one of the signs of Venus or Mars, such as Taurus, or Scorpio. As it is, you're just not one of Nature's big eaters.

You're also an air sign, as you know, and Air sign people would always rather talk than eat. You love dinner parties, and going out for a meal with your friends, but the driving impulse, as it was with your choice of car, is the social one rather than anything else. If you get into a good argument or discussion at the table you will be able to look down at your plate when everyone else has finished, and see that you haven't eaten any of it because you've been so busy talking.

The best food for Aquarians, as it is for all the air signs, is light food, things which can be eaten in a single

mouthful and which don't need much attention paying
to them on the part of the person eating. You like
buffets, and party-type food, where you can have a little
of this and a little of that, and most importantly of all,
carry on socializing while you do so. If you look at what
you choose, you may notice that you have a tendency
to go for food which is brightly coloured, especially
anything which is from the yellow-orange range of the
spectrum. The deep reds and browns of rich meats,
and the dense green of vegetables are less attractive to
you.

One good thing about your appetite is that it is very
broad; you'll eat anything. Unlike your companion
Saturn sign Capricorn, you'll happily try exotic tastes
you've never met before, and especially when you're
in company; being in a party of people going out to try
a new restaurant serving Himalayan cuisine sounds like
your idea of fun.

Holidays
Aquarians have a liking for being on their own, and yet
need to be in a crowd; they also like to be different
from anyone else, and to visit the places nobody else
has heard of.

A fortnight on a beach under a hot sun is fine as far as
it goes, and you don't really mind it as long as you are
with your friends (the need to socialize and
communicate again), but there will be times when you
will want to wander off and be on your own, as
Aquarians always do.

Capricorns like wandering off too, but whereas they
always go up into the hills to be on their own, Aquarians
wander down into the market to see what the locals are
doing. Wherever you go, you really get involved with
the local life; to you, it's what makes the place what it is.

If you think about it, you will see that it suits your
Aquarian needs perfectly. When you are in a busy
market, with all sorts of things happening around you,

you are in with the crowd and part of the action — just the sort of things you love — but at the same time, because you are the foreigner, you're separate from it, and a little different. That's the unique combination of circumstances that an Aquarian likes to feel — being part of the crowd and yet separate from it at the same time — and if you can achieve that on holiday by visiting a local town or village, then it's no wonder you like it so much.

Like all the Air signs, you have a facility for languages. You may not have known that, but you do. When you're in a foreign land you instinctively pick up the little phrases which make up day-to-day conversations, and by the time a couple of weeks have gone by, you're good enough to hear what's being said in a local bar, and to have conversations with local shopkeepers. Becoming part of the local scene is something that you like; if life on holiday was the same as being at home you wouldn't go.

In Roman times it used to be said that the sign of Aquarius was associated with the most faraway places then known, such as Scandinavia and Siberia. The places which appeal to you don't necessarily have to be cold, but they do have to be off the beaten track.

Drinks

Aquarians are great drinkers, but not for the alcohol — that's the Pisceans' department. As usual, you do it for the social aspect. A group of friends in a pub, all talking at once and with most of them involved in at least two conversations at the same time, is a very Aquarian gathering.

Being the most modern and forward-looking sign, you are more than happy to be in a pub which has been decorated in the modern style — bright lights, chrome rails, pot plants. As always, the conversation matters more to you than the decoration, so you don't mind the style as long as the company is lively. It's some of the other signs, like Taurus and Leo, who want their pubs to be full of wooden seats, old beams, and horse brasses.

If there is a specific drink which can be associated with Aquarius then it has to be lager. It can be the sort of drink to have in your hand while talking, and while not paying a great deal of attention to the drink itself, which suits Aquarians very well; and it has a sort of sociable, group-together feeling associated with it, which also matches the sign. At its best, it is cool, and has a sharpness to it, like Aquarian thinking.

Sports and pastimes

The inescapable need to be in company which guides the Aquarian in everything means that team sports can usually boast an Aquarian or two, but individual athletic disciplines are short of them.

Aquarians lack the robustness and that peculiar animal quality which makes the Fire signs (Aries, Leo, Sagittarius) so happy to get themselves covered in mud on a Saturday afternoon, though the idea of being in the thick of things with the rest of the team has a strong appeal. On the whole, Aquarians choose sports where mobility rather than strength is required, and like all the Air signs seem to do well with racquet sports such as tennis, and with badminton in particular.

Many Aquarians like to spend their spare time helping with various political or charitable activities, distributing leaflets or attending various meetings. It is unusual to find an Aquarian without some sort of favourite cause or group of this kind.

Pastimes with a technical side to them are always Aquarian favourites. During the last ten years or so, many Aquarians have taken up playing with computers in their spare time. There is always a strong attraction for you in anything scientific, so everything from amateur astronomy to building your own hi-fi will be of interest. Aquarians also have a love of machinery, of course, as mentioned earlier; restoring old cars, motorcycles, aeroplanes, in fact anything with an engine in it, is something you love.

When you have a spare moment to read a book, and it isn't something serious, like a political work or a computer manual, then you will read science fiction. You have a fondness for comics, too.

Colour and style

Aquarian style is an expression of your need for independence, to show that you are different and unique. Often, there is some element of shock in what you wear, something which is surprising and unexpected.

It isn't a shock which is intended to outrage or to attract the opposite sex, in the way that, say, a Scorpio will wear something which is very provocative, but just something to be noticed. An example of the sort of thing I mean is wearing an ordinary suit, for either sex, in a conventional style, but in a surprising colour, such as orange, where everyone might expect grey or navy.

You seem to have a liking for the more unusual colours. Orange is often associated with the sign, and so is electric blue, and all the neon colours like lime green or vivid pink. In traditional astrology, from the centuries before today's bright dyes were created, Aquarius was associated with dark blue or indigo, the colours of the night sky. Indigo is also the colour of denim when new, of course, and Aquarians seemed to be the first to take to wearing jeans for all occasions in the Sixties, as well as the last to stop doing so. Jeans were, and are, a very democratic way of dressing, because everybody, from princes to paupers, wore them, and that universal appeal is important to an Aquarian's way of thinking. There is a distinct Aquarian look, derived from working clothes, which is made up from jeans, industrial footwear, short jackets, scarves and caps, and which is often the preferred style of the

Aquarian with strong political interests.

There is also a 'scientific' Aquarian look, predominantly grey or blue, with check patterns being a noticeable feature.

Saturn's influence on the sign keeps you in fairly simple outlines; an unusual colour appeals to you, but an unusual shape, or something with a lot of extra fabric for its own sake, makes you uncomfortable. What *will* draw your eye, though, is anything with a strong diagonal line in its design, either in cut or in colour.

Aquarius is the sign most usually associated with futuristic fashion, as worn in all the best science-fiction movies, and futuristic fabrics, such as plastics. Some signs — Taurus in particular — look absolutely awful in vinyl, but Aquarians seem to suit it.

Work

It is difficult to imagine what the computer business would have done without Aquarians. The computer department of a large corporation may have over half its staff with their birthdays in the sign. The logical thinking and the rather impersonal approach that the sign gives you are perfectly matched to the requirements of computer work. Other technical and scientific work seems to attract Aquarians, too, especially in anything to do with electricity, telephones, or radio.

On a slightly larger scale, it used to be said that anything to do with railways was Aquarian, and anything to do with aviation, as well, though that might also be Sagittarian. Medical Aquarians are rare, but musical ones aren't, and there are many who work in the technical side of the recording industry, as well as a few who are performers as well. Aquarians have a particular feel for jazz and experimental music.

The other main area that Aquarians tend to cluster in is that of the social services, or working for local councils. There are a lot of Aquarian teachers, too, mostly at secondary school or college level.

It may seem like a fairly wide range of jobs, but there are certain things that they have in common, and these are the Aquarian strengths.

What you are particularly good at is putting principles into action. A problem is found, and the correct course of action is taken. What you're not so good at is the situation of, let us say, salesman, where there is bargaining to be done, and possibly a bit of a game going on, before the deal is done. That's too loose a situation for you: you are better where the rules are quite clear. One of the reasons that Aquarians enjoy technical jobs so much is that machines obey the laws of physics; they work according to the rules, and if they are not working for some reason, then that reason can be determined by logical thinking.

Where you are at your weakest is in any job where you don't know exactly what's required. If you are in a position of logical superiority then you are fine, but if you are as much in the dark as the next person, and it is quite possible that he may get the better of you by exploiting something that he knows and you don't, then you are confused and unhappy. The key to job satisfaction, for you, is complete understanding of the situation.

To sum up, things to go for:
- Any modern industry, computers or electronics;
- Any kind of work which serves or benefits the community, rather than makes profits for a commercial organization;
- Anything unusual or experimental.

Things to avoid:
- Any job which gives you no time to think, and where your ideas are unlikely to be listened to or asked for;
- Any job which works your hands harder than your brain;

- Any job where you have direct and personal responsibility for what happens, and its consequences.

People

You like people who are:
- Individual;
- Intellectual;
- Sociable.

You dislike people who are:
- Conceited;
- Over-emotional;
- Only doing what they do for the money.

PISCES

Home

A Piscean home is likely to look untidy, but there is more to it than merely being disorganized. It is like that on purpose: to have everything in its place and carefully arranged would be very upsetting to the Piscean mind. You like to be reminded, every time you come across something, of what it means to you, and you like to be surprised by things occurring where you had not expected them. It is the principle of *mixing* and *variety* which is so important to you, and your house must be able to provide that too.

Your choice of furniture is likely to be in a mixture of styles, but soft and comfortable rather than bare wood or metal. Piscean homes have lots of fabrics — curtains and carpets — thrown over things, and unusual lighting arrangements; the idea is to camouflage the rigid lines of the room, and make it hard to see where one thing ends and another begins. Mixture and variety, you see. There are lots of ornaments and pictures, and rather less in the way of practical furnishings, like clocks, but that's because emotional values and sentiments matter more to you than telling the time.

Cars

Cars are very much a feature of any modern lifestyle, but the Piscean treats them as a convenience, nothing more. You don't get terribly excited about the prospect of owning or driving one, as the Arians do, and you don't judge yourself and your own status by the size of your car, as Capricorns do. In fact, if you didn't have a car at all, that wouldn't worry you too much, and there are lots of Pisceans who manage quite happily without one.

It's important to see how far down your list of priorities a car is. You may well wonder what all the fuss is about — and that's just the point: four or five of the signs view their car as the most important thing they have, but you're not like that at all.

Above all, what you don't want is for your car to be a moving advertisement for you. You will recognize, I am sure, those people — usually from Fire signs like Aries or Leo — who want their car to be a larger, more obvious version of all the qualities in themselves of which they are so proud. They want to show themselves off to the world, and their car helps them do it. You understand this, but you don't really want to do it yourself. You want the opposite, in fact. You want as little of yourself as possible to be on display.

Nor do you need your car to be a status symbol. The Earth signs, especially Taurus and Capricorn, like to be able to touch the gleaming paintwork and the soft upholstery, and to remind themselves that they have been properly rewarded for their efforts. A new car, or a large car, is a real target in life for these people, and it should be seen more as a symbol of their success than as a means of transportation.

The things that you, as a Pisces, actually want a car to do are fairly modest. Firstly, you want it to take you where you want to go, and it doesn't have to be particularly large or expensive to do that. Note that I haven't said that it takes you from one place *to another*; far more important, to the Piscean's way of thinking, is that it takes you away from somewhere you'd rather not be. Taking you *to* somewhere is something else entirely, something you might not care to do. As always with Pisces, escape is more important than joining in.

The second thing that you want your car to do is to insulate you from everyone else. There are times when you find it rather more than you can take to be in a crowd of people. Being as sensitive as you are, there are all sorts of things which you can't help but tune in to, and which you'd rather not. You need to be alone with yourself, removed from the world, and if your car can function as a little retreat, a place where you can shut off the outside world, just for a little while, then it is a great help. You probably like driving on your own. You are quite happy to be alone with your thoughts, uninterrupted, and if you wish you can fill that little bit of private space with something else — usually music from the car's radio or tape player — to create the sort of sensations that you *like* to tune in to.

It is very important for you, as you know, to be able to slip away quietly when necessary. For this reason you are unlikely to choose any sort of a car which is too obvious or noticeable. You're quite happy with the ordinary model of anything, rather than the GTI. The reason is simple: the ordinary model is the one which never attracts a second glance, and becomes invisible in the general flow of traffic. That's precisely why it appeals to you, and of course precisely why it *doesn't* appeal to the Arians and the Leos.

The exception to this rule of not being noticed is when you find a car whose shape and emotional associations have an overwhelming appeal. There are a number of Pisceans who are attracted to old cars, but it's always because of the beauty of the car's shape, and the romantic air that so many of them have, rather than their performance, or sporting history. You are particularly keen on anything which seems to evoke a particular era or perhaps an old film; an ordinary French saloon car from the Forties or Fifties, for example. It's the mood of the times you are re-creating, not any sort of high-performance image.

Apart from these flights of fantasy, what do you choose? Anything which has more curves than straight lines, usually, and nothing which is aggressively styled, or too long in relation to its width. You prefer your cars to be light in weight, for maximum mobility, and easy to drive; a great big imposing limousine which needs a lot of effort at the wheel to make it change direction is much too much for you. You're not the physical type, and really you're looking for something which can be directed as much by thought as by muscle. It doesn't exist — yet — but when it does, you'll buy one. In colours, you avoid red because it's too noticeable, and black because it's too definite; the colours which appeal to you are greens and blues.

There seems to be a long-standing attraction between Pisceans and Renaults; particularly the older models. It may well be to do with the rounded contours of the cars, but the idea of 'invisibility' could have something to do with it, too. Anything which takes you out of trouble, gives you some space to yourself, and doesn't attract attention to you when you don't want it, is fine. Anything more is more than you want.

Food

It sounds too obvious to say that Pisceans eat fish, even if it's true. It also sounds like cannibalism, if you think about it.

You *do* eat fish, but there's more to it than that. You are a Water sign, along with Cancer and Scorpio, and so you have an association with liquids generally. You prefer food which came in liquid originally, like fish, or all the varieties of seafood, and also food which has a high water content, such as fruits and vegetables. That excludes heavy meats and things like that, which you don't enjoy so much.

Water signs enjoy smooth textures, too. Anything which has been whipped, or pureed, or creamed, is to your taste, and so are light, moist, and airy things, like soufflés and mousses. You tend to eat with your lips and tongue rather than your teeth: chewing is something you'd rather not do.

You may like your food soft, but you don't like it insipid. Rich flavours are your favourites — that's the influence of Jupiter, which runs through all Pisceans — and you are particularly fond of anything which has been cooked using either cream or some kind of alcohol, and preferably both.

The emotional associations of food are not lost on you. Some things are favourites because they remind you of a certain person or a certain place, and sometimes you will choose a certain dish or style of cooking because you want to put yourself in a certain mood. It's something you are very good at, and it means that you can enjoy a meal for more than its flavour, which the rest of us can't.

Holidays

Pisceans really do need to 'get away from it all', as the holiday brochures say. You also need to be beside the sea — and that's as far as it goes, really. The riotous social life and the pursuit of the perfect suntan have no part in your plans; what you want is to be alone by the water.

Water plays an important part on your holiday plans. Rivers, lakes, the sea — you like them to be part of your holiday environment, and you like to spend time listening to the sounds they make. The sound of water is soothing to the Piscean mind, somehow, and far more so than the babble of conversation; that's something the Gemini would find hard to understand. Lots of Pisceans like to spend time on canal boats, or sat on the riverbank fishing. It isn't through a fascination with lock gates, either, or from a desire to catch anything; it's just an excuse to be away from human contact, and to listen to the sounds of the water. Sailing is a popular Piscean pursuit, too, and for the same reasons.

Traditionally, Pisces has been associated with the great oceans; it may be that the Mediterranean, which has no tides, isn't mobile enough for you. It used to be said that the great Piscean places were those which faced the Atlantic, but there's no reason not to include the Pacific too, and perhaps the perfect Piscean retreat would be a small island in the Pacific, perfectly private, and surrounded by ocean for hundreds of miles.

The various places in the world were assigned to the zodiac signs centuries ago, and Pisces is said to be associated with Portugal, and with Normandy in France. Both of these face the Atlantic, of course. Somewhere else Piscean, or so it is said, is the Sahara desert, which is rather hard to understand. Perhaps it is the complete isolation from everywhere else which is the secret of its appeal.

Drinks

Pisceans and alcoholic liquor go together naturally. Jupiter, the planet which governs the sign, governs alcohol as well, so you can call it a Piscean substance if you like. It used to be said that Pisceans were more prone than any other sign to become alcoholics, though to be fair it used to be said of Scorpios too, and neither statement is necessarily true, of course.

What you like about drinking is quite simple, and in fact the most obvious reason of all. Alcohol changes your emotional state, and you enjoy the intensified emotions that it produces. It's as simple as that. You enjoy the social life, too, but a Pisces is a creature for

whom emotional responses are the most important
thing in life, and therefore anything which makes those
responses seem stronger will attract you. It is the same
for Taureans and food, Capricorns and money, Librans
and love; it's something that gives you more of what
you like most.

Your basic Piscean instincts are still there, though,
whenever you enter a pub. Watch what you do next
time you're in one. You always sit where you can leave
easily, or without being seen. Sometimes this means
sitting near the door. The hidden corners at the back
which are difficult to get out of are for the Scorpios and
some of the other signs, not for you.

Your choice of drinks is very broad. If it's alcoholic,
you'll drink it. A very Piscean drink which has been
enjoying something of a revival lately is Pernod; not
only is it strongly alcoholic, but the peculiar colour that
it goes when mixed with water, a sort of opalescent
milky blue, is very much a Piscean shade, and it will
have a definite appeal for you.

Sports and pastimes
Pisceans are not the athletes of the zodiac — that's the
job of the next sign, Aries. The Piscean frame is usually
too delicate to get involved in anything requiring great
strength, and your mind isn't sharp or precise enough
to really enjoy directing the rapid responses involved
in say, squash or fencing. You are much better suited to
graceful or flowing movements, as found in swimming
(but not in competition) or in dancing, at which are very
good.

Water sports of all kinds, and those associated with
water, such as fishing, attract you, but it's not the
physical activity which provides the satisfaction so
much as the relaxation and the soothing sound of the
water.

What you really enjoy doing in your spare time is
anything to do with pictures. Lots of Pisceans are film

addicts, and will happily go to the cinema two or three times a week. There are lots of Pisceans who enjoy painting, too — *water*colours for the Water sign, of course — but the biggest interest of all for Pisceans is photography.

Photography is a Piscean process from start to finish. It is about images, capturing a mood or a moment, made possible by a sensitive emulsion, developed in various chemicals. All of these things, including the chemicals, are associated with the sign of Pisces.

Lastly, Pisceans have always enjoyed the theatre, and acting is something you really like. There is a special magic about costume and scenery which brings out the best in you, and lets your powerful imagination be used to the full.

Colour and style

Piscean style is hard to pin down. It takes inspiration from everything, and manages to mix different elements in a way that nobody else could either imagine or get away with. It is usually rather theatrical, but the only definite thing which can be said about it is that it is indefinite.

You never choose anything which has a definite shape or cut to it, and certainly nothing which will present a neat, sharp silhouette. A suit with square shoulders and very clean-cut lines to it is something you'd never choose unless you absolutely had to, because it would be too straight, too limited, too well defined. You're a softer person than that, and you like your clothes to be soft and indefinite, too; big, oversized sweaters and coats which hide rather than define the shape of the wearer, and shirts which were never designed to be worn with a tie.

You like your clothes to fit loosely. Movement, or at least the ability to move when you want to, is very important to you, and you don't like the idea of wearing clothes which prevent you from moving freely; you become worried when you wear something that's too tight, because you feel that Piscean need to escape, and your clothes are trapping you.

Pisces is the sign most likely to wear clothes which don't match, and also to wear clothes in layers, so that you add more things when you get cold, and take a few off when you get hot. It's quite a sensible way of doing things, but it can give a rather disorganized look, which is of course precisely why you like it: it's *indefinite*.

You have a preference for mixed colours, and a particular fondness for the colours of the ocean; blues, greens, and any mixture of the two, through to mauves and purple. Strong primaries, like red and yellow, are uncomfortable for you, because they have such a strong effect, and you are sensitive to it. For the same reason, you often wear pale or pastel colours when you don't feel like trying very hard; you can manage them more easily.

The great Piscean advantage in fashion is that you can wear almost anything, and make it look the way that it is supposed to. You don't have a strong flavour of your own which clashes with certain styles; instead, you absorb the associations of whatever you are wearing, and to good effect. Dress sporty, and you look athletic (you *look* athletic; it doesn't mean that you *are* athletic); dress elegant and traditional, and you look aristocratic, and so on. It's like acting, in a way, and what you are doing is putting on a different role with each costume.

Finally, there is the Piscean love affair with shoes. Each part of the body is associated with a zodiac sign, and in the case of Pisces it's your feet. That's why you like your shoes to be comfortable, and why you have so many of them. They come in two kinds — the old and comfortable, and the highly fashionable. If your shoes aren't right for the occasion, then you're unhappy, and a change of shoes will often be enough to change your mood.

Work

There are about four or five career areas which seem to attract Pisceans more than any other; they don't seem to have a great deal in common, but in fact they can all be linked to the sign of Pisces quite easily.

The most obvious one is fish. Pisces is the sign of the fish, and it may surprise you to find that a great number of Pisceans manage to make a career either farming, or selling, or serving, fish. This living the sign literally seems only to apply to Pisceans, and to Sagittarians, who work with horses. The other signs don't seem to connect with their animals in the same way.

Another obvious area is alcohol. As mentioned earlier, alcohol is a Piscean substance, and there are any number of Pisceans who are publicans, or bar staff. There are also lots of Pisceans who work for the companies who manufacture, or distribute, alcoholic products.

Not far away from alcohol, and still associated with Pisces, is the chemical industry in all its branches, including the pharmaceutical industry. All drugs and chemicals are Piscean, and all paints, colourings, and dyes, too; Pisceans have a natural affinity with all of these things.

Medicine, and particularly nursing, has always been a Piscean area. The obvious specialization is to be a chiropodist, since Pisces is connected to the feet, but it is the process of nursing, especially long-term nursing, such as that of the chronically ill, the elderly, or the handicapped, which attracts more Pisceans than any other form of medicine. Only Pisces can give the care and understanding required by the long-term patient, but at the same time can withdraw when that care is more than the patient can deal with. When sympathy matters more than surgery, Pisces is the first choice.

The most glamorous Piscean occupations are in the world of the theatre, or in the media. The advertising industry, the film studios, and the record business are always keen to find creative people whose sensitivity to what is seen and heard can be turned to profitable use. Pisceans are uniquely talented in this respect; it is your feeling for what's going on in society generally which gets translated into music and fashion, and which *makes* the style of the times.

To sum up, things to go for:
- Any job which requires creative imagination, not necessarily linked to a practical result;
- Any job which requires sympathy and understanding, where person-to-person contact is important;
- Anything artistic or spiritual in content.

Things to avoid:
- Anything which involves a manual process or heavy labour;
- Anything too restricted and regimented;
- Working under high pressure or to deadlines.

People
You like people who are:
- sensitive and sympathetic;
- brilliant and glamorous;
- original thinkers.

You dislike people who:
- have no imagination;
- value things by their price alone;
- are abrupt and aggressive.

4
LOVE-HATE CHART

WHO ARE THE PEOPLE YOU *DON'T* GET ON WITH?

Most astrology books have a section in them where they say which signs are compatible with yours. That's all very well, but the thing you could really use, most of the time, is some sort of indication as to which signs you *don't* get on with, so that you know what you're in for when you are introduced to somebody for the first time. This is especially useful when you find yourself sitting opposite somebody new in the office; you're going to spend nearly half your waking day with them, five days a week, and although knowing whether you are 'compatible' is all very well if you are trying to marry them, it's not a great deal of use if you're trying to make some sort of a working relationship.

Here, then, is something a little different — a table of the signs which tells you how well, or how badly, they get on with each other. The higher the score, the more arguments the pair of you are likely to have; the lower the score, the easier it will be for the pair of you to get along — though both of you may sometimes need a kick in the rear to get you moving.

You are likely to be most interested in the scores which apply to your own sign, of course, but the other signs are all included so that you can have some fun working out what your friends are having to deal with in their own relationships. Not only is this great fun, but it enables you to be as nosy as you like without anyone knowing!

Of course, this chart works for *all* relationships, not just romances, and not just for male-female, either. So, you can use it to find out why you keep arguing with your father, your sister, even your boss; it tells you the truth about all of them.

How to use the chart

It couldn't be easier. Find your own sign going down the left hand column, then read across to find how you score

THEM YOU	Aries	Taurus	Gemini	Cancer	Leo	Virgo	Libra	Scorpio	Sagittarius	Capricorn	Aquarius	Pisces
Aries	6	9	2	7	3	7	4	6	3	5	2	8
Taurus	9	6	8	2	6	4	6	4	7	3	6	1
Gemini	2	8	5	8	2	4	3	7	4	7	3	8
Cancer	6	1	8	5	8	2	6	6	7	4	7	3
Leo	2	6	2	7	5	7	3	4	3	7	4	7
Virgo	7	3	5	2	8	4	8	2	7	3	7	5
Libra	4	6	3	6	2	9	5	9	2	6	3	6
Scorpio	6	4	7	4	6	2	9	6	8	1	6	3
Sagittarius	3	7	4	6	3	7	2	8	5	9	2	5
Capricorn	7	3	7	4	8	3	5	2	8	6	5	3
Aquarius	3	6	3	8	4	7	2	6	2	7	5	8
Pisces	8	2	7	2	7	4	7	3	5	3	8	5

Love-Hate Chart

with another person from each of the twelve signs.

Make sure you remember which one is you and which one is the other person, because the answer isn't the same in both directions. For example, a Leo gets a score of 2 with an Aries, but the Aries gets a score of 3 with a Leo. This means that the Leo finds the Aries slightly easier to get on with than the Aries finds the Leo, and so if there are any arguments it will usually be the Aries who starts them, and the Aries who loses his temper first.

INTERPRETING THE SCORES

Score 1   *Too Easy.*
This is the relationship with almost no friction at all in it. The two of you understand each other's point of view perfectly, and you know instinctively what to do to please each other. At times, you are almost the same person, because it is very easy for you to make the slight changes to your opinions and tastes which will bring you into perfect alignment. The trouble with this arrangement is that relationships actually work better if there's a little bit of friction, so that each partner can bring out the best of the other, and so that each of you can do things that you wouldn't have tried if you had been on your own. With this relationship it isn't like that, though, because you are so close; what happens instead is that you let yourselves get lazy, and you both slip back into your old bad habits, doing the sort of things that you know you shouldn't.

Score 2   *Very Easy.*
This is the 'best-of-friends' relationship, where the two of you get on very well and really enjoy each other's company. It's usually a very talkative relationship, where the two of you find that you have endless things to talk about, and love nothing better than to sit with

each other over a drink, and to lay out all your dreams and plans for the future. It doesn't matter that none of these plans ever seem to be put into action, or that you change them from day to day; you just enjoy being with each other, and you *like* each other. It's as simple as that. You don't have arguments very often, firstly because you like each other too much, and secondly because this is a light and mobile relationship, and disagreement seems too heavy a thing to bring into it. If there are areas where you don't meet eye-to-eye, then you simply pass them by and talk about something else. There's always something new to talk about, so why cause unpleasantness?

Score 3   *Easy.*
This is the relationship where each partner finds qualities in the other which he really admires, and wishes he had in himself. When you are with this person, you are constantly hoping that by being with them, some of their style, sense of humour, confidence, or whatever, will rub off on you. Whenever they do something, you find yourself thinking, 'That's really good, I wish I'd thought of that.' It's not all one-way traffic, though; in fact, the two of you show off and reflect each other's talents very well, so it brings out the best in both of you. The only time that you argue is when one of you thinks that the other is doing something in a way that you *wouldn't* like to copy. You will find yourself saying, 'I wish you wouldn't do that!' Think about why you say that: what you wish is that they'd do it in a way that you would like to do it yourself. Luckily, it doesn't happen often; most of the time this pairing reminds you of all the things you like best about yourself and can see in the other person.

Score 4   *Variable.*
This is where the major differences start to creep in. With this score, there are going to be an increasing

number of occasions when the two of you seem to hold exactly opposite views on how best to do something. It's quite funny to watch, for an outsider, because your views aren't actually very different — just opposite. In practice, it means that the relationship goes up and down a bit; sometimes you both do things your way, and sometimes your partner's way. What you have going for you is that you share the same basic outlook on life, and the things that are really important to you are important to both of you. You don't have to go round trying to explain the way you feel to somebody who seems to have no comprehension of what you're on about. There is a tendency for the pair of you to have similar weaknesses, which makes it difficult for one to help the other, but that's true to some extent for all the low-score relationships.

Score 5 *Brisk, workable.*

This is the half-way score, balanced between perfect alignment and constant conflict. There are likely to be a fair number of arguments with this relationship, but they won't last long, and they are usually productive, in that they release frustrations, help communication, and stimulate growth. Most of the combinations which produce a score of 5 are from two people of the same sign, and those that aren't are from signs which have other factors in common. This means that there is a great deal of *understanding* with this score; you may not like what the other person does all of the time, but you can understand why he feels the way he does, because you would feel that way yourself if you were in his or her shoes. You never get the feeling that this person is something very alien to you, somebody whose soul you can never hope to understand. This familiarity means that you can accept your differences with a grin and a shrug of the shoulders. You forgive each other, but you know that there will be more arguments some-time in the future. You don't mind: you'd still rather have this person as a friend than some others you could think of.

Score 6 *Challenging.*

With this relationship the differences start to become more obvious than the similarities, and you realize quite early on that you are two different people who need to develop a system of give and take if you are to get along together. In fact, things could be much worse, and you are usually able to recognize in each other the strengths and talents that you yourself don't have. You will also notice that you are both successful in your own areas, each in ways that the other just couldn't manage. Following on from this comes a sort of admiration for each other's differences, and you start to defend each other when necessary, as in 'He may not be very ambitious, but he's very kind and considerate, and I like that.' If you don't learn to appreciate each other's strengths, you simply criticize each other for being different, and the relationship never gets a chance to grow. If you both give your talents to the relationship, and don't interfere in each other's areas unless asked, this can be a very strong and successful union.

Score 7 *Adjustment needed.*

This score usually indicates a relationship where the two people are so different that they are unlikely to have any points of contact. That's not necessarily a bad thing, because at least you leave each other alone to get on with what you have to do, but it does mean that you have to make positive and determined efforts to form a relationship; you can't just muddle along and hope that something will grow, because it probably won't. You are essentially separate people, with separate aims and interests, and that makes it very difficult for you even to understand, let alone appreciate or share, what the other person is trying to do. You will have to try to understand how they see things, try to put yourself in their position, and try to see what they are aiming for. It's not easy, for either of you, but if you *can* bridge the gap in any way you will be able to help each other out and solve each other's problems in ways that you wouldn't have imagined possible. It's a real long-term commitment, this one, and it's not for the selfish or the lazy.

Score 8   *Difficult.*
The appealing thing about a relationship like this, especially at the beginning, is the very high level of involvement. You just don't seem to be able to ignore each other, and that's an encouraging start. You just don't seem to be able to agree on anything, either, but you keep trying, because you both believe that you're right, and that with just a little more persuasion the other person will be able to see your point of view and come over to your side. In fact, it seldom gets any better, and you could easily stay like that, arguing back and forth forever. Much of the problem comes from an absolute refusal to do things any way but your own, and you feel that to even try things their way just once would be letting them win, and you won't have that. It's a pity that this relationship boils down to being a simple contest in so many cases; what it highlights is the lack of confidence each person has in himself. If you can stop fighting for a moment, and believe that you won't somehow die by doing things *their* way, you will be able to see how much they have to offer you that you need and can't do for yourself.

Score 9   *Extremely difficult.*
This score is thankfully rare, and is only possible with certain combinations of signs which are next to each other. What makes 9 different from an 8 is that the other person's viewpoint and way of working specifically blocks your own, so that not only are your actions in conflict with his, but his actions prevent you from

functioning properly by taking away the very things you need most. The result is that you feel completely unable to be yourself, and that makes you depressed. Either you let yourself be completely controlled and ordered by them, which is a bad thing, or you have massive confrontations every so often where you demand the freedom, or the space, or whatever it is, to be yourself and to feel happy and contented. After a while they will close in on you again, and you will have to fight for your space once more; the process will go on and on. To make this one work you must learn to live in the same space without treading on each other. If you can do that, the relationship can be quiet, safe and long-lasting; if you can't, you'll destroy each other.

5
FACES AND BODIES

Being the sign you are involves more than just ways of thinking and feeling — it influences the way you look, too. The twelve zodiac signs each have a set of physical features associated with them, and your birthday will determine which set you get to wear

Over the last couple of thousand years, astrologers have spent a lot of time matching faces to birthdays and to times of birth, and have produced descriptions which are not just linked to the month of your birth, but to the day or the hour as well. Once you know your way round them, you will be able to see not only how closely *you* fit the pattern, but spot others in your sign as well.

Here are the basic types; see how many of the key features of your sign match your own.

ARIES

General outline:
Trim, balanced, lean. The Arian frame isn't particularly broad but it isn't thin and elongated as, say, a Virgo's. It seems well-proportioned, and the upper and lower halves of the body are balanced, so that if the upper half is well-built then the lower half will be the same. The frame is very strong: big bones are covered in muscle and sinew, but very little extra tissue, and there's not usually a lot of extra weight to carry.

Height:
Taller than average, seldom very short.

Hair:
Traditionally supposed to be reddish and wiry;
certainly the sign seems to put reddish tones into
whatever colour the hair is.

Complexion:
Well-coloured, sometimes flushed; almost never pale
or clear.

Distinguishing features:
The posture of an Arian is unmistakable; there's no
slump or roundedness. It's as though all the internal
slack has been taken up, and the muscles are holding
all the limbs in light tension, so that they don't flop
around. The head is always held up, with the face
upturned towards whatever's coming next; Arians
don't look at the ground. The general posture is
upright, but tends to lean forwards, almost as though
running, and when walking there is an athletic
briskness to the process, with arms swinging to help
maintain momentum. Some signs dawdle, but Arians
march.

Face:
The Arian face is made of short straight lines, clear-cut
and distinctive. This isn't a round face, with soft
features, but rather a triangular construction, with its
widest point at the eyes. Some Arian faces are longer
than others, but they all finish in a fairly narrow chin,
which prevents the face ever seeming square. The
eyes are set behind strong brows, and are usually blue
or grey; very dark eyes are rare in an Arian. It is
obvious that they are an instrument for actively looking
rather than passively seeing — they are sharp and
observant, and it shows.

TAURUS

General outline:
Rectangular. Whatever the height, the overall impression is never narrow, because the whole frame is broad and solid, which sometimes gives an impression of being even shorter than is in fact the case. The Taurean body is solid, but it isn't necessarily fat.

The upper half of the body is much broader and stronger than the lower half, so Taureans are broad across the back and shoulders but relatively narrow in the hips.

Height:
Medium to short, seldom very tall.

Hair:
Traditionally supposed to be dark and curly.

Complexion:
Brownish or reddish, not often very fair. Skin ages well, tans well, doesn't get dry.

Distinguishing features:
The set of the head is noticeable. A Taurean head is set slightly forward and down, and the neck is short and very strong — just like the Bull which is the animal of the sign! The muscles at the back of the neck, going out into the shoulders, are very pronounced in Taurean men. Hands are usually large, squarish in shape, with short fingers.

Face:
Like the body, quite broad, so that even if it is long it never seems narrow. The forehead is wide and flat. Most of the features are wide, in fact, and the mouth is very full, never thin and mean. The eyes are large, but kindly and sympathetic, not hard or wide and staring.

Gemini

General outline:
Narrow. The whole body seems to be much longer than it is wide, although that doesn't necessarily mean thin. The body is quite well balanced in that the shoulders and the hips are about the same size, and so instead of seeing a round outline, or a triangular one, the onlooker sees a sort of vertical rectangle. Some very ancient authorities, however, thought that this sign tended to emphasize the hips and thighs.

The body is carried lightly, as though it weighed very little. Posture is good, very upright, and there is no stoop or curve. Geminis are light on their feet, too, almost skipping as they walk.

Height:
Tall, in almost all cases.

Hair:
Traditionally supposed to be dark brown or black.

Complexion:
Well-coloured, sometimes rather yellowish or olive in complexion.

Distinguishing features:
The most noticeable thing about Geminis is that they talk — unceasingly, and about anything and everything. The voice is usually light, and speech is extremely rapid. There are a lot of arm and hand movements to aid communication; note that the arms (and legs) are often long, but the hands don't match them; Gemini hands are short and rather square in many cases.

Face:
The Gemini face is usually rather long. The forehead is noticeable, with very prominent temples; often the

hairline starts well back on the head, leaving the forehead area full and rounded. This is particularly easy to see on Gemini men as they get older and their hair starts to recede. The features are small, and rather sharp-looking, almost pointed; this includes the nose, but a Gemini nose is often *small* and pointed, rather than being a curved or Roman nose. The eyes are small, but very alert, and they sparkle as the Gemini speaks, particularly when he is telling a story, as is often the case. The eyes of Gemini women are supposed to be the most attractive in the zodiac.

CANCER

General outline:
Rather short and round. The weight on a Cancerian seems to be centred in the body rather than the limbs, and it is rare for the sign to have well-developed shoulders or thighs. The upper half of the body seems to be larger than the lower half, but this is only because the weight is in the torso and the arms and legs are shorter than in other signs. Muscle tone isn't apparent; the body may not actually be fat, but the flesh always appears soft. It is very easy for the Cancerian physique to put on weight, usually round the waist and on the abdomen.

Height:
Medium to short, seldom very tall.

Hair:
Traditionally supposed to be fine and delicate, a light brown colour, but rather lacking in body.

Complexion:
Always said to be pale, almost white. Very little cheek colour. Texture not as smooth as some, and tends to have blemishes.

Distinguishing features:
Overall *roundness*. The face is very round, almost a genuine circle. The body appears round, especially if the person is slightly overweight, and the set of the shoulders is round too. Even the arms are held in a slight curve, rather than fully straightened, when walking.

Face:
Very round, with the features set quite closely together in the middle of it. Eyes are said to be grey, but at any rate are not often of a very dark colour. The jawline is indistinct, and the cheekbones are not prominent; this is a *soft* face.

LEO

General outline:
Rectangular. Whatever the height, the overall impression is never narrow, because the whole frame is broad across the shoulders, and the torso is usually full and deep as well. The lower half of the body is much slimmer. The physique is actually like the lion of the sign — big at the shoulder, deep chested, narrow hipped. The body is well-muscled, but it is usually possible to see where the bones are, all the same; again, like a lion or some other big cat.

Height:
Medium to tall, seldom very short.

Hair:
Traditionally supposed to be a golden mane, rather stiff and bushy; it stands off the head before sweeping back in luxuriant profusion. Some authorities say, however, that male Leos lose their hair quickly with age.

Complexion:
Reddish, with a high colour, and sometimes rather an angry appearance.

Distinguishing features:
The way a Leo carries himself is his most easily identifiable feature. Every Leo walks as tall as he can, with his back straight, his chest out, and his head up. There is never a slouch or a stoop, and the posture is always one of confidence; Leos look the world straight in the eye, sure of their own position.

Face:
A Leo face is broad and rounded, though not as circular as the Cancerian's. The features are 'handsome'; that is, they are large and generously formed, well-spaced, not narrow or close together. The forehead is broad and flat, and the eyes look out from under it; sometimes this can make the eyes look as though they are staring, or that the person is constantly angry.

VIRGO

General outline:
Long and narrow. The accent in the Virgo outline is always on the *vertical* rather than the horizontal; it is the length of the limbs or the length of the face which seem to be noticed first. Many Virgos are indeed quite thin, since the sign has no tendency to gain weight or to store fat, but even those who are as broad as the rest of us always *seem* to be leaner.

No part of the Virgo physique ever seems large: big feet and hands, that sort of thing, belong to other signs.

Height:
Medium. Tall Virgoans are not uncommon, but short ones are rare.

Hair:
Traditionally supposed to be mid to dark brown,
perhaps even black, and extremely straight, with no
hint of a curl or a wave.

Complexion:
Ancient authorities say that it tends towards the colour
of someone with a tan. It seems that Virgoan
complexions contain colours from the yellow-orange-
brown part of the spectrum rather than the white-pink-
rose range, which is more Libran.

Distinguishing features:
The most noticeable thing about a Virgoan is the
distance between the waist and the hips. More than any
other sign, this one is long-bodied, and so gains height
without necessarily having long legs.

Face:
Usually a long oval, quite elegant, with a high forehead.
The features on a Virgoan face are all small and can be
rather narrow; it is a pity that a small mouth is
considered less attractive these days than it used to be.
The nose is usually long, with a well-defined bridge;
sometimes the nose and chin are rather pointed. The
eyes are usually lighter in colour than complexion or
hair colour might lead you to expect.

LIBRA

General outline:
The Libran outline is long and slim. The overall
impression of the body shape is of either a long
rectangle or a graceful oval. It is unusual for the Libran
frame to be stout or bulky; there is very little
unnecessary weight. The other extreme, being thin and
rather bony, is also rare; Libran bodies are slim, but
with enough flesh to make the contours into curves, so

that the appearance is never angular. The weight distribution is good, too; the top half of the body is the same size as the lower half, and the two sides match, too. Everything about the Libran frame is *balanced*; there is never too much of this or too little of that.

Height:
Medium to tall; not often short.

Hair:
Traditionally supposed to be blonde, with a slight wave to it, and to be full and glossy.

Complexion:
Fair, ranging from white through to peach and pink. skin very delicate, sometimes prone to blemishes with increasing age.

Distinguishing features:
The most noticeable thing about Librans is their graceful motion. They are light on their feet, and very, very mobile, seeming to move the whole body through a series of gentle curves as they walk. They will often swing their hips, or their head, from side to side as they move, but it's a dance rather than a clumsy rolling movement. Everything about the Libran physique is easy on the eye — there's nothing which looks discordant or ugly.

Face:
Libran faces are the prettiest in the zodiac; all the features are well-formed and attractive. The forehead is tall and rounded, matched exactly by the shape of the lower half of the face, so that the eyes are in the precise centre, the nose is small, but straight, and the lips are full. One noticeable Libran set of features is the 'angelic' face, where the eyes are large, the nose is small, and the mouth is small but full.

SCORPIO

General outline:

Rectangular. Whatever the height, the overall impression is never narrow, because the whole frame is broad and solid. The weight seems to be concentrated in the body rather than in the arms and legs, and in the lower rather than in the upper half; this, and the fact that the legs are often rather short, gives an impression of being shorter than is actually the case.

The Scorpio body is heavy, though most of the weight is muscle rather than fat. The body movements are powerful, but restrained: a Scorpio never moves more than is necessary.

Height:

Medium to short, seldom very tall.

Hair:

Traditionally supposed to be dark and either curly or wiry.

Complexion:

Brownish or reddish, not often very fair. Often a rather 'Mediterranean' appearance.

Distinguishing features:

The most obvious thing about a Scorpio is the sense of concentrated power which surrounds them. They appear to be *concentrating* on living; the mouth will be firm, the brows set in a little frown. It is always possible to see little hints of a darker, more dangerous animal beneath the surface of a Scorpio, such as slightly unruly hair, strong hands which are slightly too large to be in proportion, or an apparently friendly smile with a wicked glint to it.

Face:

Large, rather square in shape, and often fleshy round

the neck and throat. The features are well-formed, and the mouth is full and sensuous. The most striking feature, however, are the eyes, which have an unforgettable intensity of gaze, often upsetting to others. In colour they are usually dark, going from dark browns and grey-greens to almost black, but it is the penetrating quality of their look which is the Scorpio's most noticeable feature.

SAGITTARIUS

General outline:
Long. Sagittarius gives the longest limbs in the whole zodiac, especially the legs, but it isn't as thin and narrow-looking as the Virgo or the Gemini physique, so although the length of the frame is noticeable, it doesn't look short of muscle. It's an athletic frame, but not as densely muscled or as powerful across the shoulders as the Arian or Taurean. The head is long like the rest of the body, and is carried high; this, too, makes the shoulders seem less broad. Sometimes there is a stoop, caused by years of talking to people of shorter stature and ducking through low doorways.

Height:
Medium to tall, sometimes very tall.

Hair:
Traditionally, light to mid brown. It should be strong in growth and glossy. There is a tendency for a high hairline, often unkindly referred to as 'receding'.

Complexion:
Healthy-looking, with a good colour, not often pale. Sometimes rather flushed, with strong colour in the cheeks.

Distinguishing features:
The mobility of the body is noticeable. There is a looseness to the movements which suggests that the Sagittarian is not paying much attention to his posture or to where he is putting his hands and his feet. Some signs look very tightly-knit and rather rigid, but not this one. Sagittarians are constantly on the move, unable to stay still for long; they walk well, but sit awkwardly.

Face:
Like the body, the face is quite long. The Sagittarian face has often been compared to that of a horse, and there is some truth in it. The nose is prominent, firm and straight, and the eyes are wide but kindly, taking a friendly interest in everything that happens. The mouth is full and broad, but the length of the face prevents it from appearing either too fleshy or in any way lascivious.

CAPRICORN

General outline:
Lean, but not particularly thin or narrow. Capricorns have a sort of compact, almost condensed look to them, as though they have been made with as little material as possible so as not to waste any. It is always possible to see the way the bones form the structure — there is neither a lot of fat, nor a lot of muscles on a Capricorn frame. This needn't be inelegant, though sometimes the neck and upper part of the torso look a little undernourished.

Height:
Medium, seldom very tall.

Hair:
Traditionally supposed to be dark and rather sparse, and with rather a poor texture.

Complexion:

Pale or sallow, occasionally dark. Whatever the colour, it always seems to be from the yellow-beige end of the range, and to be short of red and pink. The skin itself can be oily, but ages well, and doesn't dry out.

Distinguishing features:

There is often a twist somewhere in the Capricorn physique; sometimes one shoulder is much higher than the other, or one knee is slightly askew so that the walk is imbalanced. All the body movements are rather stiff, and defensive; broad gestures and easy, elegant motion belong to other signs. Hand and foot movements are short and rather clipped; speech is emphasized with little jabs which come from the wrist rather than the shoulder, while the walk is a quick trot which comes from the knee rather than the hip.

Face:

Strong but lean, rather serious in appearance. The jaw is firm and well-defined, and so are the cheekbones, which are easily visible, making Capricorn women attractive in a rather severe way. The eyes are usually dark in colour, and show little emotion. The nose is neat but strong, showing the bone, as ever with this sign, while the mouth often has a pronounced downward turn at the corners, even when smiling.

AQUARIUS

General outline:

Long, sometimes rather angular, but not round. The Aquarian frame is light, but quite strong. It manages to avoid being thin and rather fragile-looking, which is sometimes the case with the other Air signs such as Libra, and at the other extreme manages to avoid being overweight, and too strongly muscled to move quickly. Aquarius moves more easily than Capricorn, despite the influence of heavy Saturn in both signs. The body outline is usually quite angular — square shoulders, head held high, back held straight — but the fluency of motion save it from looking inelegant.

Height:
Medium to tall, seldom very short.

Hair:
Traditionally supposed to be dark or sandy, but there is also a strain of Aquarius which has very fine, very blond hair, almost white.

Complexion:
Fair, but well-coloured and healthy-looking. The skin is renowned for its clarity; rough texture, or blemishes, are unusual in this sign.

Distinguishing features:
There is a noticeable lightness to everything about the Aquarian, and a sense of balance, too. Aquarians seem to walk lightly, as though they don't weigh much, yet they don't look insubstantial. Everything about them seems cleaner of line, better defined, less blurred, somehow, than it is in others, and the overall impression is one of freshness, but without being sharp. Also noticeable is the way that an Aquarian always manages to keep himself to himself; unlike those signs who are always bumping into people and objects, the Aquarian only touches those things he intends to.

Face:
The general appearance is neither too light nor too dark, and in no way obscured; the whole face is clear and open-looking. Yet, because no one feature dominates, the face is often unremarkable, and

perhaps difficult to remember. Eyes are traditionally
hazel, though in very fair Aquarians they may be blue,
and the nose, which is straight but not too prominent, is
often neatly blunted at the tip.

PISCES

General outline:
Rounded, and rather bottom-heavy. Whereas Aries, the
first sign of the zodiac, gives an outline which is broad
in the shoulders and narrow in the hips, Pisces, the last
sign, reverses the emphasis. There are no sharp
corners or straight lines in the Piscean frame, either, so
the body never looks bony or thin. The body tissue is
rather soft; muscle and sinew aren't what this sign is
about. A Piscean isn't necessarily fat, but this is a body
which finds it easy to put on weight, especially on the
hips and thighs.

Height:
Medium to short, seldom very tall.

Hair:
Traditionally supposed to be soft, wavy, and dark
brown in colour. It is frequently worn long; for some
reason it seems unable to hold a cut or style.

Complexion:
Soft, delicate; colouring often very pale.

Distinguishing features:
There is a general lack of firmness in a Piscean, a sort
of floppiness as if the frame which stiffens other people
and gives them their upright posture were somehow
missing. The arms and legs are rather short compared
to the body, and the shoulders have a definite slope.
Pisceans find it difficult to keep their heads up when

they walk, and the walk itself may well be clumsy or prone to stumbling.

Face:
A Piscean head is often wider at the bottom than it is at the top, with a tendency to double chins if at all overweight. The face itself is rounded, and rather pale, with the dominant feature being the eyes, which are large and rather sleepy-looking, perhaps drooping downwards a little at their outer corners. The eyebrows are usually full and fine, to complement the large eyes. The nose is small, but the mouth is full, soft, and expressive — giving an overall effect which is romantic, but sometimes rather sad.

RISING SIGNS

Describing your physique from your Sun sign is all very well, but you probably have a couple of friends who look quite different from you, even though they have birthdays only a few days away from yours. This is because the biggest influence on the way you look comes from your rising sign. The rising sign is the one which was rising on the Eastern horizon when you were born. During the 24 hours of your birthday all twelve signs will have risen at some time or other, giving twelve different sorts of person. You might be an Aquarian, for example, if you were born in early February; but if you were born just after sunrise you might be a Pisces-type Aquarian, while someone born on the same day some hours later could be a Gemini-type Aquarian, and look very different. The difference comes through the different signs which were rising at various times during that day.

Working out your Ascendant, or rising sign, is quite a complex process, since it involves both birth date and birth time, and latitude and longitude, too; but with a few short cuts and a calculator it need only take a few minutes.

Here is the simplest routine ever devised for you to calculate your own Ascendant, provided that you know your time of birth. Pencil your answers alongside the stages as you go, so you know where you are.

1. Count forwards from the start of your sign to your birthday: e.g. for Pisces, 20 February is 1, 21 February is 2, and so on. Total days: . . . . . (max. 31)

2. Add to this the number by your sign:

Aries	183	Leo	304	Sagittarius	61
Taurus	213	Virgo	334	Capricorn	92
Gemini	243	Libra	1	Aquarius	122
Cancer	273	Scorpio	31	Pisces	152

   New total is: . . . . . (max. 365)

3. Divide by 365, and then:

4. Multiply by 24. Answer is now: . . . . . .
   (Your answer by now is between 0 and 24. If it isn't, you have made a mistake somewhere. Go back and try again).

5. Add your time of birth, in 24-hour clock time. If you were born at 3 p.m. that means 15. If you were born in Daylight Saving/Summer Time, make the necessary correction to give the true time. If there are some spare minutes, your calculator would probably like them in decimals, so it's 0.1 of an hour for each six minutes. 5.36 p.m. is 17.6, for example. Try to be as close as you can. New total is: . . . . . .

6. Astrologers always work in Greenwich Mean Time, so if you live outside the UK you probably need to add some more hours to your total. The correction for the USA, for example, is as follows:

If you were born in PST, add 8 hours to your total;
If you were born in MST, add 7 hours to your total;
If you were born in CST, add 6 hours to your total;
If you were born in EST, add 5 hours to your total.
The correction for Australia and New Zealand goes the other way:

If you were born in Perth, subtract 8 hours from your total;
If you were born in Sydney, subtract 10 hours from your total;
If you were born in Wellington, subtract 12 hours from your total.

7. Nearly finished now. Outside Britain you will need to subtract four minutes for each degree of longitude West of Greenwich. For example, if you were born in New York, which is 74°W, then you subtract 74 x 4 minutes, which is 296 minutes, or 4 hours and 56 minutes (4.93 hours if you're doing it all in decimals). If you were born East of Greenwich, then you should *add* four minutes per degree. Sydney is 151°10' East, so add 151°10' x 4, which is 604 minutes 40 seconds, or ten hours 4 minutes 40 seconds (10.077 in decimals).

8. If your total exceeds 24, subtract 24. Your answer must now be between 0 and 24. Answer is: . . . . .

9. If you were born in the Southern hemisphere, add 12 hours. This has nothing to do with time zones; it's to invert the skies to take account of the fact that you see them from the other direction. If your total exceeds 24, subtract 24 so that your answer is still between 0 and 24. Answer is: . . . . .

10. You have now got the time of your birth not in clock time, but in sidereal (or star) time, which is what astrologers work in. Pages 220 and 221 have two

diagrams, one for Northern and one for Southern latitudes, with latitudes plotted against the signs of the zodiac. Along the horizontal axis are the values 0 to 24 in Sidereal Time. Look against the time you have just calculated, and against the latitudes of the place where you were born, and you will see which sign was rising at the time and place you were born. For example, if your calculated answer is 13.6 or there-abouts, and you were born in Florida, then you have Capricorn rising, but if you were born further North, in New England, then you have the late degrees of Sagittarius rising instead. Latitude can make quite a difference, as you can see. If it looks as though in your case you could be one of two signs, then read the descriptions given and see which one fits you best.

Aries rising

With Aries rising you get height, even if the Sun sign is a 'short' one. You also get a characteristic 'fiery' look in the eyes, a sort of flash or sparkle, which shows a lively and challenging spirit. The eyebrows become larger, too, and the eyes themselves more deep-set. The face is less broad at the bottom, and becomes a sort of triangle, wide at the top, and with a pointed chin.

With this rising sign there is almost no body fat at all. The frame is athletic, fit and flat rather than curvaceous.

The real giveaway to Aries rising is the tremendous sense of energy. There is always movement; you tend to lean forward all the time, as though running because you are so eager to get started. With Aries rising you speak in short sentences, and you don't waste time with idle gossip — you are decisive, and to the point.

Taurus rising

Taurus rising gives all the broad, solid build which makes the Sun sign famous, and will add weight and solidity to the upper part of the body. The face gains

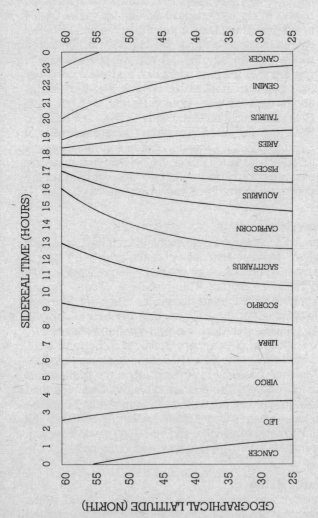

Chart I: Northern latitudes

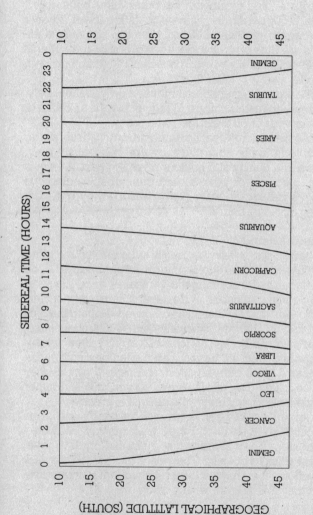

SIDEREAL TIME (HOURS)

GEOGRAPHICAL LATITUDE (SOUTH)

Chart II: Southern latitudes

soft features — soft enough even to give dimpled cheeks — and the mouth becomes fuller but smaller, with the upper lip the same size as the lower, to give the cherub's mouth of Cupid. With this sort of face the eyes are blue or brown, not often green or grey. Hair is thick and naturally wavy. The face is rather square, with a wide jaw.

The Taurus rising person moves slowly, deliberately, and never rushes things. When sitting, he is relaxed, not nervous or on the edge of the seat.

The really noticeable thing about Taurus rising people is the feeling that they are generously built, made to a quality and not to a price. No part of them is thin, pinched, or sparse, and their deep, melodious voices reflect the very real pleasure they get from living in such a frame.

Gemini rising

To have this sign rising is usually to be thinner and more slightly built than the Sun sign might suggest. The predominant direction is the vertical — in no places is this person particularly wide, though some very ancient authorities thought that this sign gave weight to the hips and thighs. The face is usually long, with long features, especially the nose. The forehead is very pronounced, and is both high and round, with the temples noticeable. Eyes are small but very alert, and have a glint as they notice things. The whole face is very mobile and rather sharp-looking, with many changes of expression.

Gemini rising people wave their hands and arms about a great deal, and they walk quickly but with a light step. They are always, it seems, on the move, never relaxed or static. They talk a lot, too, and they ask questions; they have a general air of being inquisitive, and they like to know what's going on.

Cancer rising

The noticeable thing about the appearance of anyone

with Cancer rising is how *round* they are, like the Full Moon. The face is almost a circle to look at, with the features set in the middle of what seems like a great expanse and looking rather small. There don't seem to be any firm lines in the face; the jawline is indistinct, and the chiselled cheekbones that characterize other signs just aren't there. Complexion is often rather pale, and the colour of the eyes too; it's as though all the colouring were somehow diluted, made weaker, by having Cancer rising. The hair, too, is usually fairer in colour than, say, parents or family might lead you to expect.

With Cancer rising the body is bigger than the limbs, and can be a bit flabby. The arms and legs tend to be short and a bit thin. It's not a muscular sign, so the firmness of signs like Aries isn't there. These people put on extra weight easily, especially the men, though they're not heavy in their movements.

Leo rising

Leo rising produces an unmistakable physique. The face is broad and handsome, but not fat, because the bone structure is usually visible. The whole head seems to have been built on a generous scale, and no feature is small or narrow. The forehead in particular is both broad and high, and the eyes look out with confidence and clarity from beneath heroic brows. The head is always carried high and level. Leo rising people face their world unruffled and unafraid; they don't look away shyly, screw up their eyes, look at the ground, stand with their heads bowed, or anything like that at all. There is a sort of golden glow to the face, often from the colour of the complexion or the hair, though not entirely. The hair is often golden yellow, and the desire for it to be so is strong enough to tempt those with darker hair to colour it until the golden mane is achieved. And that word 'mane' is just right, because the hair seems to stand off the head for about an inch or so before sweeping back. Leo hair is never limp or straight; it has *body*, and again those few whose hair lacks this quality will style and treat it so that it appears to have it.

All Leo rising people are as tall as they can be. They walk with their head up, their shoulders back, and their spine straight; they never ever stoop or slouch. The overall impression of someone with Leo rising is of confidence and superiority, all overlaid with that recognizable 'goldenness'.

Virgo rising
Your ears are likely to tell you that someone has Virgo rising before your eyes do. With Virgo rising, the voice becomes very penetrating. It is traditionally supposed to be thin or shrill, but other factors in the horoscope may modify this. Whatever its tone, though, it seems to cut through whatever else is going on — music, conversation — and be the voice you can't help but hear. .

Facially, Virgo rising gives a narrow face, rather pointed at times, and certainly with pointed features quite common, such as the nose or chin. No part of the face is heavy, and neither is any feature particularly large.

There is a sort of light-brownishness to Virgo rising, which affects hair and eye colour: extremes of fair and dark colouring aren't usually found with this sign rising.

The physique is narrow, even willowy, with a very long waist in many cases; breadth and bulk, either from muscle or from fat, don't seem to go with this sign. There is a noticeable neatness, even fussiness, about Virgo rising, which is quite easy to spot because these people are forever fidgeting, putting things straight and picking at this and that.

Libra rising
With Libra rising the most obvious thing is how easy on

the eye everything is. The face and the figure are both balanced and even, with nothing too big, too small, out of balance or out of proportion. The forehead is high, but not too broad, and is balanced by the lower half of the face, which matches its shape, so that an even effect is achieved. Though the face is rounded (no pointed features or heavy bones), it isn't circular, and so the overall impression is an attractive oval.

Some Libra rising people have 'angelic' features, in that they have large round eyes, small but full lips, and a small nose. The general tendency with the Libran face is for everything to be round and soft anyway; one thing that this face isn't — in any way — is rugged.

The influence of the planet Venus gives a certain elegance, a grace of movement to the body. It's quite difficult to find someone with Libra rising who is heavy-footed or clumsy, though their elegance isn't the sort of thing you notice until you look for it.

Scorpio rising

Here the physique is rather small, even if the Sun sign position suggests the opposite. Small doesn't mean light, though; the body can be quite broad, and in any case it seems to be quite heavy for its size. Some of the weight is muscle, because Scorpio rising produces quite a powerful body, but some of it is fat, and this sign puts on weight quite easily. The shoulder and neck area is often well-developed, but a narrow waist is uncommon, so the body outline is more of a cone than an hourglass.

Facially, the most obvious thing about Scorpio rising is the intensity of the gaze. To be eye to eye with someone with Scorpio rising is sometimes a disconcerting experience. The eyes are usually very dark in colour, and set wide and deep beneath a very strong brow and forehead. The overall impression of the face is that it is immensely strong and rather dangerous. The jawline is well-defined, especially in men, but the features are often soft and full. Colouring tends towards the darker end of the available range, and a pale complexion is very rare.

Sagittarius rising

Sagittarius as a rising sign gives length to the whole frame, but not at the expense of breadth or form, so the overall effect is larger and more athletic, but without ever being too narrow or too fleshy. In particular, the long bones of the legs are made larger, so that the person becomes very tall, especially if the Sun sign encourages it.

Unsurprisingly, for the sign of the centaur, there is something of the horse in Sagittarius rising, and it can be seen in the face as much as anywhere else. The forehead is both tall and broad, and the nose is long, though it is usually also straight and 'classical'. The cheekbones are often prominent, adding to the impression of leanness and length. The mouth is often quite large, and with full lips. The overall impression is one of kindly intelligence coupled with a sort of animal likeability and innocence, rather like favourite horses and dogs have.

People with Sagittarius rising are seldom still. They move with long strides, often rather gracelessly, and there is an untidiness to them which suggests that they have never quite managed to master the body they live in.

Capricorn rising

Capricorn rising makes the body leaner and bonier, and probably shorter, too, whatever the Sun sign. The shoulders seem to stick out, and the head is worn slightly forwards, between them, bowed forwards a little. It's quite difficult to get these people to stand up straight, and they lean forwards again when they walk.

Facially, Capricorn rising gives a very visible bone structure, which can be very attractive, though looking a little cold. The jaw is strongly developed, and may be rather heavy, with lines in the face to emphasize it. Many of the facial features, particularly the corners of the mouth and eyes, point downwards, and remain that way even in laughter, which is quite easy to spot. The skin is pale, and is likely to be in the cream to yellow range of complexion colours rather than the pinks or golden tones.

Movements and gestures are stiff and restricted, as much as is necessary and no more. The overall impression of the person is of someone who takes life rather seriously, and doesn't expect to enjoy it much.

Aquarius rising

The most distinctive characteristic in the appearance given by this sign rising is how clean-cut and clear all the features become. The features and physique given by the Sun sign aren't altered much at all, but somehow all the ill-defined or slightly sloppy elements get removed, and the result is a much cleaner and lighter look altogether. Aquarius rising emphasizes the vertical rather the horizontal dimension, but it doesn't make anyone too tall or too thin — just slimmer.

The face is usually a narrow oval, and the complexion is noticeably clear. The features are neat and regular, never large enough to dominate the face. There is traditionally a hint of reddish-brown somewhere in the sign, giving sandy hair or hazel eyes from time to time.

If you watch these people, you will notice that they seldom touch anything with any part of themselves unless they intend to. Some people blunder down the street bumping into almost everything, but Aquarius rising people seem to be able to keep themselves apart from all that; they have a distinct *separateness*.

Pisces rising

Pisces rising gives the least firm outline of all the signs.

Often the weight is concentrated in the lower half of the body, or even of the individual limbs, and the shoulders are quite rounded. Weight gain is easy for this sign, and it often seems to go on in all the wrong places. The strong framework of the body and the musculature which holds it in shape, seem to be entirely absent in this case. Movement, which relies on muscles, is frequently rather clumsy.

The predominant facial feature tends to be the eyes, which can be heavy-lidded and rather sleepy looking, but not unattractive. The complexion is pale, as is the eye colour too — traditionally pale blue or green. The mouth is often very soft and full, and since the face is often large and soft anyway, double chins come quite easily.

The whole person seems not to have been designed for strength or sustained effort, and it's the general lack of robustness which is perhaps the most noticeable thing.

6

THE TRUTH ABOUT BEING BORN *ON THE CUSP*

Life can sometimes be confusing if your birthday is at the end of the third week of the month. In one magazine, for example, it will say that Aries starts on March 20th, but in another it will say that Aries starts on the 21st, and that anyone who was born on the 20th is a late Piscean.

'But I don't feel like my sign!' you cry, 'I feel like the next one!' The answer you usually get is that you were born *on the cusp*, a mysterious area where the Sun is neither one sign nor the other, and where the qualities of both signs can be found mingled together.

It's a good word, *cusp*. It's the sort of word you'd never find outside astrology, so you go away with ideas of it meaning some sort of grey area where two things are possible at once, a place where you can be either, or both, of two zodiacal characters. It's nothing of the sort, actually. The word cusp means a *point*, a *tip*; the Sun changes from one sign into the next at a single point in time, and there is never a time when it is in both at once. There is no vague area where they join — you're either one or the other, and that's that.

So why do magazines tell you all this stuff about cusps? Why do they move the dates around?

Well, actually, it's a white lie, to save having to go into a long explanation, and because it used to be thought that nobody really wanted to know. But it seems that everybody with a birthday anywhere near the change of signs really does want to know which one they really are — so here is the real answer.

It's all to do with the calendar. On a calendar the year is 365 days long, but the Sun isn't so neat in making its annual trip round the zodiac; it takes 365 days, 5 hours, 48 minutes, and 46 seconds. The calendar catches up the difference by having an extra day every four years, making a leap year, and it makes further fine tuning by *not* having leap years at the ends of the centuries unless the number is divisible by 400. It still isn't quite right, but it's quite good, and it will be a few thousand years yet before the difference is enough for us to worry about.

The trouble comes when you try and fix a position from one system to the other. The first moment of a sign may be on the 21st one year, but it may be on the 22nd the next. Those spare five hours and all the minutes and seconds may take you forward into the early hours of the next day. Then there's the leap year to consider, and a few other things besides. It's a tricky business.

Magazine astrologers have two choices; either they could take an average date, like the 20th, and accept that for some years they will be wrong, or they could print a whole list of years and times so that the readers could sort out for themselves which sign they really were. Such a list (times twelve, of course, for all the signs) would take up a great deal of space, so that's why they don't do it. They go for the average date option, instead. Sometimes they pick the 20th, and sometimes the 21st, but it really doesn't matter; the dates are only there as a guide.

But here, for people who really want to know, is the other option — tables of the dates and the times when the Sun went into Aries, and when it went out into Taurus, and so on, so now you check which one you really are, and which horoscopes you should be reading in your favourite magazine. It may mean, of course, that you discover that you are not what you thought after all!

The times in this table are in GMT, so that if you were born outside the UK, you can adjust for the time zone difference. In the UK, you will have to allow for the seasonal variations — Summer Time, for which you will have to take an hour off your birth time to get GMT, and in some years Double Summer Time, for which two hours must be taken off. Notes on this follow at the bottom of each table.

INTO ARIES

Year	Date (March)	time
1940[1]	20th	18.24
1941[1]	21st	00.20
1942[2]	21st	06.11
1943[2]	21st	12.03
1944[2]	20th	17.49
1945[2]	20th	23.37
1946	21st	05.33
1947[2]	21st	11.13
1948	20th	16.57
1949	20th	22.48
1950	21st	04.35
1951	21st	10.26
1952	20th	16.14
1953	20th	22.01
1954	21st	03.53
1955	21st	09.35
1956[3]	20th	15.20
1957	20th	21.17
1958	21st	03.06
1959	21st	08.55
1960	20th	14.43
1961	20th	20.32
1962	21st	02.30
1963	21st	08.20
1964	20th	14.10
1965	20th	20.05
1966	21st	01.53
1967	21st	07.37

Year	Date (March)	time
1968[1]	20th	13.22
1969[1]	20th	19.03
1970[1]	21st	00.57
1971[1]	21st	06.38
1972	20th	12.22
1973	20th	18.13
1974	21st	00.07
1975	21st	05.57
1976	20th	11.50
1977	20th	17.43
1978	20th	23.34
1979	21st	05.22
1980	20th	11.10
1981	20th	17.03
1982	20th	22.56
1983	21st	04.39
1984	20th	10.25
1985	20th	16.14
1986	20th	22.03
1987	21st	03.52
1988	20th	09.39
1989	20th	15.29
1990	20th	21.20
1991	21st	03.02
1992	20th	08.49
1993	20th	14.41
1994	20th	20.28
1995	21st	02.15

Except where indicated, the start of Aries in the UK is usually in GMT, and the end, when it passes into Taurus, is usually in Summer Time.
[1] Summer Time throughout Aries period.
[2] Summer Time throughout Aries period, and Double Summer Time by end of Aries period.
[3] GMT throughout Aries period.

INTO TAURUS

Year	Date (April)	time	Year	Date (April)	time
1940	20th	05.51	1968	20th	00.41
1941[1]	20th	11.50	1969	20th	06.27
1942[2]	20th	17.39	1970	20th	12.15
1943[2]	20th	23.31	1971	20th	17.54
1944[2]	20th	05.18	1972	19th	23.38
1945[2]	20th	11.07	1973	20th	05.30
1946	20th	17.02	1974	20th	11.19
1947[2]	20th	22.39	1975	20th	17.07
1948	20th	04.25	1976	19th	23.03
1949	20th	10.17	1977	20th	04.57
1950	20th	15.59	1978	20th	10.50
1951	20th	21.48	1979	20th	16.35
1952	20th	03.37	1980	19th	22.23
1953	20th	09.25	1981	20th	04.19
1954	20th	15.19	1982	20th	10.08
1955	20th	20.58	1983	20th	15.50
1956[3]	20th	02.43	1984	19th	21.38
1957	20th	08.41	1985	20th	03.26
1958	20th	14.27	1986	20th	09.12
1959	20th	20.17	1987	20th	14.58
1960	20th	02.06	1988	19th	20.45
1961	20th	07.55	1989	20th	02.39
1962	20th	13.51	1990	20th	08.27
1963	20th	19.36	1991	20th	14.09
1964	20th	01.27	1992	19th	19.57
1965	20th	07.26	1993	20th	01.49
1966	20th	13.12	1994	20th	07.36
1967	20th	18.55	1995	20th	13.22

In the UK, Taureans are almost always born in Summer Time — the exceptions are:

[1] Double Summer Time at end of Taurus period.
[2] Double Summer Time throughout.
[3] Not Summer Time until 22nd, 02.00.

INTO GEMINI

Year	Date (May)	time		Year	Date (May)	time
1940	21st	05.23		1968	21st	00.06
1941[1]	21st	11.23		1969	21st	05.50
1942[1]	21st	17.08		1970	21st	11.37
1943[1]	21st	23.03		1971	21st	17.15
1944[1]	21st	04.51		1972	20th	22.59
1945[1]	21st	10.40		1973	21st	04.54
1946	21st	16.34		1974	21st	10.36
1947[1]	21st	22.09		1975	21st	16.24
1948	21st	03.57		1976	20th	22.21
1949	21st	09.50		1977	21st	04.14
1950	21st	15.27		1978	21st	10.08
1951	21st	21.15		1979	21st	15.54
1952	21st	03.04		1980	20th	21.42
1953	21st	08.53		1981	21st	03.39
1954	21st	14.47		1982	21st	09.23
1955	21st	20.24		1983	21st	15.07
1956	21st	02.12		1984	20th	20.58
1957	21st	08.10		1985	21st	02.43
1958	21st	13.51		1986	21st	08.28
1959	21st	19.42		1987	21st	14.10
1960	21st	01.33		1988	20th	19.57
1961	21st	07.22		1989	21st	01.54
1962	21st	13.16		1990	21st	07.37
1963	21st	18.58		1991	21st	13.20
1964	21st	00.50		1992	20th	19.12
1965	21st	06.50		1993	21st	01.02
1966	21st	12.32		1994	21st	06.49
1967	21st	18.18		1995	21st	12.34

In the UK, Geminis are usually born in Summer Time, except:
[1] Double Summer Time in these years.

INTO CANCER

Year	Date (June)	time	Year	Date (June)	time
1940	21st	13.36	1968	21st	08.13
1941[1]	21st	19.33	1969	21st	13.56
1942[1]	22nd	01.16	1970	21st	19.43
1943[1]	22nd	07.12	1971	22nd	01.20
1944[1]	21st	13.02	1972	21st	07.06
1945[1]	21st	18.52	1973	21st	13.01
1946	22nd	00.44	1974	21st	18.38
1947[1]	22nd	06.19	1975	22nd	00.27
1948	21st	12.11	1976	21st	06.25
1949	21st	18.03	1977	21st	12.14
1950	21st	23.36	1978	21st	18.10
1951	22nd	05.25	1979	21st	23.57
1952	21st	11.13	1980	21st	05.47
1953	21st	17.00	1981	21st	11.45
1954	21st	22.54	1982	21st	17.43
1955	22nd	04.31	1983	21st	23.09
1956	21st	10.24	1984	21st	05.03
1957	21st	16.21	1985	21st	10.45
1958	21st	21.57	1986	21st	16.30
1959	22nd	03.50	1987	21st	22.11
1960	21st	09.42	1988	21st	03.57
1961	21st	15.30	1989	21st	09.53
1962	21st	21.54	1990	21st	15.33
1963	22nd	03.04	1991	21st	21.19
1964	21st	08.57	1992	21st	03.15
1965	21st	14.56	1993	21st	09.00
1966	21st	20.34	1994	21st	14.48
1967	22nd	02.23	1995	21st	20.34

In the UK, Cancerians are usually born in Summer Time, except:
[1] Double Summer Time in these years.

INTO LEO

Year	Date (July)	time	Year	Date (July)	time
1940	23rd	00.34	1968	22nd	19.08
1941[1]	23rd	06.26	1969	23rd	00.48
1942[1]	23rd	12.07	1970	23rd	06.37
1943[1]	23rd	18.04	1971	23rd	12.15
1944[1]	22nd	23.56	1972	22nd	18.03
1945[1]	23rd	05.45	1973	22nd	23.56
1946	23rd	11.37	1974	23rd	05.30
1947[1]	23rd	17.14	1975	23rd	11.22
1948	22nd	23.08	1976	22nd	17.19
1949	23rd	04.57	1977	22nd	23.04
1950	23rd	10.30	1978	23rd	05.01
1951	23rd	16.21	1979	23rd	10.49
1952	22nd	22.07	1980	22nd	16.42
1953	23rd	03.52	1981	22nd	22.40
1954	23rd	09.45	1982	23rd	04.16
1955	23rd	15.25	1983	23rd	10.05
1956	22nd	21.20	1984	22nd	15.59
1957	23rd	03.15	1985	22nd	21.37
1958	23rd	08.51	1986	23rd	03.25
1959	23rd	14.46	1987	23rd	09.06
1960	22nd	20.38	1988	22nd	14.52
1961	23rd	02.24	1989	22nd	20.46
1962	23rd	08.18	1990	23rd	02.22
1963	23rd	13.59	1991	23rd	08.12
1964	22nd	19.53	1992	22nd	14.09
1965	23rd	01.48	1993	22nd	19.51
1966	23rd	07.23	1994	23rd	01.41
1967	23rd	13.16	1995	23rd	07.30

In the UK, Leos are usually born in Summer Time, except:
[1] Double Summer Time in these years.

INTO VIRGO

Year	Date (August)	time
1940[1]	23rd	07.28
1941[1]	23rd	13.17
1942[1]	23rd	18.58
1943[1]	24th	00.55
1944[1]	23rd	06.46
1945[1]	23rd	12.35
1946	23rd	18.26
1947[1]	24th	00.09
1948	23rd	06.03
1949	23rd	11.48
1950	23rd	17.23
1951	23rd	23.16
1952	23rd	05.03
1953	23rd	10.45
1954	23rd	16.36
1955	23rd	22.19
1956	23rd	04.15
1957	23rd	10.08
1958	23rd	15.46
1959	23rd	21.44
1960	23rd	03.34
1961	23rd	09.19
1962	23rd	15.13
1963	23rd	20.58
1964	23rd	02.51
1965	23rd	08.43
1966	23rd	14.18
1967	23rd	20.13

Year	Date (August)	time
1968[1]	23rd	02.03
1969	23rd	07.44
1970	23rd	13.34
1971	23rd	19.15
1972	23rd	01.03
1973	23rd	06.54
1974	23rd	12.29
1975	23rd	18.24
1976	23rd	00.19
1977	23rd	06.01
1978	23rd	11.57
1979	23rd	17.47
1980	22nd	23.41
1981	23rd	05.39
1982	23rd	11.16
1983	23rd	17.08
1984	22nd	23.01
1985	23rd	04.36
1986	23rd	10.26
1987	23rd	16.10
1988	22nd	21.54
1989	23rd	03.47
1990	23rd	09.21
1991	23rd	15.13
1992	22nd	21.11
1993	23rd	02.51
1994	23rd	08.44
1995	23rd	14.35

In the UK, Virgos are usually born in Summer Time, except:
[1] Double Summer Time in these years.

INTO LIBRA

Year	Date (September)	time	Year	Date (September)	time
1940[1]	23rd	04.46	1968	22nd	23.26
1941[1]	23rd	10.33	1969	23rd	05.07
1942[1]	23rd	16.16	1970	23rd	10.59
1943[1]	23rd	22.16	1971	23rd	16.45
1944[1]	23rd	04.02	1972	22nd	22.33
1945[1]	23rd	09.50	1973	23rd	04.21
1946	23rd	15.41	1974	23rd	09.59
1947[1]	23rd	21.29	1975	23rd	15.55
1948	23rd	03.22	1976	22nd	21.48
1949	23rd	09.06	1977	23rd	03.30
1950	23rd	14.44	1978	23rd	09.26
1951	23rd	20.37	1979	23rd	15.17
1952	23rd	02.24	1980	22nd	21.09
1953	23rd	08.06	1981	23rd	03.06
1954	23rd	13.55	1982	23rd	08.47
1955	23rd	19.41	1983	23rd	14.42
1956	23rd	01.35	1984	22nd	20.33
1957	23rd	07.26	1985	23rd	02.08
1958	23rd	13.09	1986	23rd	07.59
1959	23rd	19.09	1987	23rd	13.46
1960	23rd	00.59	1988	22nd	19.29
1961	23rd	06.43	1989	23rd	01.20
1962	23rd	12.35	1990	23rd	06.56
1963	23rd	18.24	1991	23rd	12.49
1964	23rd	00.17	1992	22nd	18.43
1965	23rd	06.06	1993	23rd	00.23
1966	23rd	11.43	1994	23rd	06.19
1967	23rd	17.38	1995	23rd	12.13

In the UK, Libras are usually born in Summer Time. The years when the end of Libra was *not* in Summer Time were 1945–6, 1953–60, 1977 and 1983.

[1] Double Summer Time in these years.

INTO SCORPIO

Year	Date (October)	time	Year	Date (October)	time
1940[1]	23rd	13.39	1968[1]	23rd	08.30
1941[1]	23rd	19.27	1969[1]	23rd	14.11
1942[1]	24th	01.15	1970[1]	23rd	20.04
1943[1]	24th	07.08	1971[1]	24th	01.53
1944[1]	23rd	12.58	1972	23rd	07.42
1945[1]	23rd	18.44	1973	23rd	13.30
1946	24th	00.35	1974	23rd	19.11
1947[1]	24th	06.26	1975	24th	01.06
1948	23rd	12.18	1976	23rd	06.58
1949	23rd	18.03	1977	23rd	12.41
1950	23rd	23.45	1978	23rd	18.37
1951	24th	05.35	1979	24th	00.28
1952	23rd	11.22	1980	23rd	06.18
1953	23rd	17.06	1981	23rd	12.13
1954	23rd	22.56	1982	23rd	17.58
1955	24th	04.43	1983	23rd	23.55
1956	23rd	10.34	1984	23rd	05.46
1957	23rd	16.24	1985	23rd	11.22
1958	23rd	22.11	1986	23rd	17.15
1959	24th	04.11	1987	23rd	23.01
1960	23rd	10.02	1988	23rd	04.45
1961	23rd	15.47	1989	23rd	10.36
1962	23rd	21.40	1990	23rd	16.14
1963	24th	03.29	1991	23rd	22.06
1964	23rd	09.21	1992	23rd	03.58
1965	23rd	15.10	1993	23rd	09.38
1966	23rd	20.51	1994	23rd	15.36
1967	24th	02.44	1995	23rd	21.32

In the UK, Scorpios are usually born outside Summer Time, but in most years the clocks were still forward at the very beginning of Scorpio. The start of Scorpio was not in Summer Time in 1945, 1950–60, 1966, 1977, 1983, 1988 (and probably 1993 too).

[1] Summer Time all year round in the UK in these years.

INTO SAGITTARIUS

Year	Date (November)	time		Year	Date (November)	time
1940[1]	22nd	10.49		1968[1]	22nd	05.49
1941[1]	22nd	16.48		1969[1]	22nd	11.31
1942[1]	22nd	22.30		1970[1]	22nd	17.25
1943[1]	23rd	04.21		1971[1]	22nd	23.14
1944[1]	22nd	10.08		1972	22nd	05.03
1945	22nd	15.55		1973	22nd	10.54
1946	22nd	21.46		1974	22nd	16.39
1947	23rd	03.38		1975	22nd	22.31
1948	22nd	09.29		1976	22nd	04.22
1949	22nd	15.16		1977	22nd	10.07
1950	22nd	21.03		1978	22nd	16.05
1951	23rd	02.51		1979	22nd	21.54
1952	22nd	08.36		1980	22nd	03.42
1953	22nd	14.22		1981	22nd	09.36
1954	22nd	20.14		1982	22nd	15.24
1955	23rd	02.01		1983	22nd	21.19
1956	22nd	07.50		1984	22nd	03.11
1957	22nd	13.39		1985	22nd	08.51
1958	22nd	19.29		1986	22nd	14.45
1959	23rd	01.27		1987	22nd	20.30
1960	22nd	07.18		1988	22nd	02.12
1961	22nd	13.08		1989	22nd	08.05
1962	22nd	19.02		1990	22nd	13.47
1963	23rd	00.49		1991	22nd	19.36
1964	22nd	06.39		1992	22nd	01.26
1965	22nd	12.29		1993	22nd	07.07
1966	22nd	18.14		1994	22nd	13.06
1967	23rd	00.05		1995	22nd	19.02

In the UK, there was *permanent* Summer Time in 1940–44 and 1968–71, so:
[1] Time one hour ahead of GMT all year round in the UK in these years.

INTO CAPRICORN

Year	Date (December)	time
1940[2]	21st	23.55
1941[1]	22nd	05.44
1942[1]	22nd	11.40
1943[1]	22nd	17.29
1944[1]	21st	23.15
1945	22nd	05.04
1946	22nd	10.53
1947	22nd	16.43
1948	21st	22.33
1949	22nd	04.23
1950	22nd	10.13
1951	22nd	16.00
1952	21st	21.43
1953	22nd	03.31
1954	22nd	09.24
1955	22nd	15.11
1956	21st	21.00
1957	22nd	02.49
1958	22nd	08.40
1959	22nd	14.34
1960	21st	20.26
1961	22nd	02.20
1962	22nd	08.15
1963	22nd	14.02
1964	21st	19.50
1965	22nd	01.41
1966	22nd	07.28
1967	22nd	13.16

Year	Date (December)	time
1968[2]	21st	19.00
1969[1]	22nd	00.44
1970[1]	22nd	06.36
1971[1]	22nd	12.24
1972	21st	18.13
1973	22nd	00.08
1974	22nd	05.56
1975	22nd	11.46
1976	21st	17.35
1977	21st	23.23
1978	22nd	05.21
1979	22nd	11.10
1980	21st	16.56
1981	21st	22.51
1982	22nd	04.39
1983	22nd	10.30
1984	21st	16.23
1985	21st	22.08
1986	22nd	04.03
1987	22nd	09.46
1988	21st	15.28
1989	21st	21.22
1990	22nd	03.07
1991	22nd	08.54
1992	21st	14.44
1993	21st	20.26
1994	22nd	02.23
1995	22nd	08.17

In the UK, there was *permanent* Summer Time in 1940–44 and 1968–71, so:

[1] Time one hour ahead of GMT all year round in the UK in these years.

[2] Time one hour ahead of GMT by December in this year, but not in January.

INTO AQUARIUS

Year	Date (January)	time
1940[1]	21st	04.44
1941[1]	20th	10.34
1942[1]	20th	16.23
1943[1]	20th	22.19
1944[1]	21st	04.07
1945	20th	09.54
1946	20th	15.45
1947	20th	21.32
1948	21st	03.18
1949	20th	09.09
1950	20th	15.00
1951	20th	20.52
1952	21st	02.38
1953	20th	08.21
1954	20th	14.11
1955	20th	20.02
1956	21st	01.48
1957	20th	07.39
1958	20th	13.29
1959	20th	19.19
1960	21st	01.10
1961	20th	07.01
1962	20th	12.58
1963	20th	18.54
1964	21st	00.41
1965	20th	06.29
1966	20th	12.20
1967	20th	18.08

Year	Date (January)	time
1968[2]	20th	23.54
1969[1]	20th	05.38
1970[1]	20th	11.54
1971[1]	20th	17.13
1972	20th	22.59
1973	20th	04.48
1974	20th	10.46
1975	20th	16.37
1976	20th	22.25
1977	20th	04.15
1978	20th	10.14
1979	20th	16.00
1980	20th	21.49
1981	20th	03.36
1982	20th	09.31
1983	20th	15.17
1984	20th	21.05
1985	20th	02.58
1986	20th	08.47
1987	20th	14.41
1988	20th	20.25
1989	20th	02.07
1990	20th	08.02
1991	20th	13.48
1992	20th	19.38
1993	20th	01.23
1994	20th	07.08
1995	20th	13.01

In the UK, there was *permanent* Summer Time from 1941–44 and from 1968–71, so:

[1] Time one hour ahead of GMT all year round in the UK in these years.

[2] Time one hour ahead of GMT started 18th February in this year.

INTO PISCES

Year	Date (February)	time		Year	Date (February)	time
1940[2]	19th	19.04		1968[1]	19th	14.09
1941[1]	19th	00.56		1969[1]	18th	19.55
1942[1]	19th	06.47		1970[1]	19th	01.42
1943[1]	19th	12.40		1971[1]	19th	07.27
1944[1]	19th	18.27		1972[2]	19th	13.12
1945[1]	19th	00.15		1973[2]	18th	19.01
1946	19th	06.09		1974[2]	19th	00.59
1947[1]	19th	11.52		1975[2]	19th	06.50
1948[1]	19th	17.37		1976	19th	12.40
1949	18th	23.27		1977[2]	18th	18.31
1950	19th	05.18		1978[2]	19th	00.21
1951	19th	11.10		1979[2]	19th	06.14
1952	19th	16.57		1980[2]	19th	12.02
1953	18th	22.41		1981	18th	17.52
1954	19th	04.32		1982	18th	23.47
1955	19th	10.19		1983	19th	05.31
1956	19th	16.05		1984	19th	11.17
1957	18th	21.58		1985	18th	17.08
1958	19th	03.49		1986	18th	22.58
1959	19th	09.38		1987	19th	04.50
1960	19th	15.26		1988	19th	10.36
1961	18th	21.17		1989	18th	16.21
1962	19th	03.15		1990	18th	22.14
1963	19th	09.09		1991	19th	03.59
1964	19th	14.57		1992	19th	09.44
1965	18th	20.48		1993	18th	15.36
1966[2]	19th	02.38		1994	18th	21.22
1967[2]	19th	08.24		1995	19th	03.11

In the UK, Summer Time often begins just as Pisces changes to Aries, and years when this could be a deciding factor are marked accordingly. Also, during 1941–44 and 1968–71, there was *permanent* Summer Time.

[1] Time one hour ahead of GMT throughout Pisces period in the UK in these years.

[2] Time one hour ahead of GMT by end of Pisces period in the UK in these years.

7
WHO SHARES YOUR BIRTHDAY?

It's fun to see who else shares your birthday. Anybody who shares your birthday, or is within a day of it (for the reason why you can be a day each side, see 'The Truth About Being Born *On The Cusp*' on page 229) will represent the same degree of the zodiac as you do, and that means that although you won't necessarily look like them, you will be similar in character. Just *think* — nobody will know what somebody famous is *really* like, but you will, because you share a birthday with them. They're just like you, in lots of ways.

ARIES

Aries is supposedly the sign of soldiers and sportsmen, but it's musicians who seem to belong to the early part of the sign: Bach had his birthday on the 21st, and Andrew Lloyd Webber on the 22nd. The sportsmen make an appearance on the 23rd, with Roger Bannister, the first man to run a mile in less than four minutes.

Two interior designers next: William Morris on the 24th, and David Hicks on the 25th, which is also Elton John's birthday. Diana Ross is close to Elton on the 26th, and she shares *her* birthday with Leonard

Nimoy, of *Star Trek* fame. The end of March also seems to have produced some of the greatest early movie stars, with Fatty Arbuckle on the 24th, Gloria Swanson on the 27th, and Lon Chaney Sr on April 1st.

March 28th is interesting, since both Neil Kinnock and Norman Tebbit have their birthdays then, and so does Michael Parkinson. David Steel, for so long the leader of the Liberal Party, isn't far away from his political colleagues, either — his birthday is on the 31st. In between those two dates come two very famous Arian artists, both born on the 30th: Goya and Van Gogh.

Tony Benn, another politician, celebrates on April 3rd. So does Marlon Brando, and one of Hollywood's newest stars, Eddie Murphy. Two stars from an earlier movie era share the 5th, too: Bette Davis, and Spencer Tracy.

A most unusual Arian, but certainly someone who used his physical capabilities to the full, had his birthday on April 6th — Houdini. And also on the 6th, the Dutch aviation pioneer Anthony Fokker, whose name is still on aircraft to this day.

The poet Wordsworth was born on April 7th, and so was someone else who knows what words are worth — David Frost. And on the subject of frost, the ice skater Sonja Henie, the Olympic champion who later became a film star, was born on April 8th.

Staying with Arian athleticism, but moving from skating to golf, we get Severiano Ballesteros, whose birthday is April 9th. There's yet another star from the pioneer days of Hollywood here, too — Mary Pickford — and another poet, the Frenchman Charles Baudelaire. He may just possibly have been the most Arian Arian who ever lived; not only did he have the Sun in Aries, as you do, but Venus, Mars, Jupiter, and Saturn in Aries as well. How would *you* like to be five times as much of yourself?

The middle of April seems to be a bit short of names from the pages of history, apart from a renowned murderer or two, but the 15th means celebrations for two people who are never far from the public eye: Jeffrey Archer and Samantha Fox.

For some reason April 16th seems to produce men of comic genius: Spike Milligan, Charlie Chaplin, and Peter Ustinov were all born on this date.

Aries bows out with a great conductor: Leopold Stokowski, who you may remember is the conductor of the orchestra in Walt Disney's *Fantasia* — his birthday was on April 18th.

TAURUS

Any very early Taurean, with a birthday on the 20th, shares his birthday with Hitler, but most Taureans prefer to associate themselves instead with the birthday of the Queen, which is on the 21st. So was Charlotte Brontë's, for literature fans. The 22nd is the day for the violinist Yehudi Menuhin, and George Cole, of *Minder* fame, while the following day, St George's Day, is Shakespeare's birthday.

Taurean affinity with the voice seems to be prominent on the 24th and 25th, with Barbra Streisand and Ella Fitzgerald as examples, but there's also royal photographer Patrick Litchfield. Young Royals seem to proliferate in this part of the zodiac: Lady Helen Windsor is a 28th April Taurus, and Lady Sarah Armstrong-Jones has her birthday on 1st May.

Queen of the May, with her birthday on the 1st, is Joanna Lumley, and then come another rush of singers: Bing Crosby on the 2nd, Tammy Wynette on the 4th, and some others, not so well-known.

The middle of the sign has the heavyweights, both in

body and in influence: Henry Cooper on the 3rd, Karl Marx on the 5th, Orson Welles on the 6th, and Sigmund Freud, grandfather of psychoanalysis, also on the 6th. Fans of Hollywood's golden years may like to remember Tyrone Power on the 5th, and Rudolph Valentino, the great screen lover, on the 6th. And one explorer, too, also on the 6th: Robert Peary, first man to reach the North Pole.

May 7th is extraordinarily cultured, so if you like music you're in good company here: both Brahms and Tchaikovsky were born on this day, and so was Robert Browning, the poet.

President Truman, the man who took the decision to drop the atomic bomb, and who invented the phrase 'the buck stops here', was born on May 8th. A fine example of Taurean firmness and practicality; but what does that say about David Attenborough, the naturalist, who shares the 8th with him?

It seems to be theatre day on the 9th, in the same way as it was music day on the 7th; Albert Finney, Glenda Jackson, and playwright Alan Bennett all celebrate now.

Salvador Dali, the famous surrealist painter, has his birthday on the 11th. Two cool women, both objects of adoration in their day, come next, only a day apart, on the 12th and 13th: Florence Nightingale and Selina Scott. And two musicians on the 13th, as well: Sir Arthur Sullivan, Gilbert's partner, and Stevie Wonder. There's another pianist on the 16th, too: Liberace.

The final week of Taurus has some intriguing mixtures of birthday sharers. Toyah Wilcox and Fred Perry, the tennis player whose shirts everyone knows, share the 18th, which was also the birthday of the last czar, Nicholas II. Pete Townsend and Victoria Wood share the 19th, and bringing up the rear, slow but reliable like so many of the parts he's played, is Hollywood actor James Stewart, whose birthday is the 20th.

GEMINI

Gemini is supposed to be the sign of the greatest ingenuity, and with an affinity for the written word; it's very satisfying to find Sir Arthur Conan Doyle opening the list of Geminis with his birthday on 22nd May. His greatest and most lasting creation, Sherlock Holmes, is a perfect Gemini in every detail — and was played in many Hollywood versions of the Holmes stories by Basil Rathbone, who was also a Gemini (13th June).

May Geminis seem attracted to Hollywood: Douglas Fairbanks Snr was born on the 23rd, as was Joan Collins, and two old companions of the horror movies, Peter Cushing and Vincent Price, are a day apart on the 26th and the 27th. Cushing, of course, has played Sherlock Holmes from time to time, as well. John Wayne, also on the 26th, shows how tall Geminis can get, as does the similarly sized Clint Eastwood, whose birthday is the 31st.

Only a day later, on 1st June, comes Marilyn Monroe, herself a day away from the most famous Tarzan of them all. Johnny Weissmuller, whose birthday is the 2nd. At the other end of the sign on 20th June, but still tall, dark, and dashing, as Geminis all should be, comes Errol Flynn.

It's not just the kings and queens of Hollywood who are Geminis; real royalty seems to like the sign as well. Queen Victoria was a triple Gemini, with both the Sun and the moon in Gemini, as well as Gemini rising (see page 216); her birthday was 24th May. King George V was a 3rd June Gemini, while Queen Mary, his consort, had her birthday just over a week earlier on 26th May. Alexandra, last empress of Russia, was born on 6th June; her daughter Anastasia, last of the Romanovs, kept the sign in the family by arriving on the 17th. And Royal Geminis are still going strong, with Prince Philip celebrating on 10th June. Finally, Wallis Simpson, the

Duchess of Windsor, was also a Gemini; her birthday was 19th June.

There seems to be quite a number of Geminis in music and literature. Thomas Hardy and Thomas Mann were born on 2nd and 6th June. Hollywood's legendary columnist Hedda Hopper shared Hardy's birthday, and so did the Marquis de Sade! The dancer Isadora Duncan was born on 27th May, one day before Ian Fleming, the creator of James Bond. Amongst the composers, Wagner comes earliest in the sign, up on 22nd May; he is followed three weeks later by Richard Strauss, whose birthday was 11th June. Between them zodiacally, but not musically, comes Schumann, whose birthday was the 8th. Modern musicians seem set to continue Gemini's involvement with the world of music through Paul McCartney, born on 18th June.

12th June seems to produce politicians: Sir Anthony Eden, Prime Minister during the 1950's, had his birthday then, and so does George Bush.

Whilst thinking of America, which is a Gemini nation despite being born on 4th July (it has the Sun in Cancer, but *Gemini* rising), it's worth noting that its most quoted philosopher, Emerson, was born on 25th May, while its most famous president, John F. Kennedy, was born on the 29th.

Last of all, not zodiacally but alphabetically, is a poet: W. B. Yeats. His birthday was 13th June.

CANCER

The newest famous Cancerian is Prince William, who was born when the Sun had been in Cancer for only a few hours.

Cancer is a sign connected with ideas of womanhood, the emotions, and patriotic pride, and the early days of the sign seem to excel themselves in producing people who show these qualities. 22nd June, in particular, seems to provide women of definite, though different, character: Esther Rantzen, Meryl Streep, Cindi Lauper. The Duke of Windsor, whose birthday was the 23rd, had to solve the uniquely Cancerian problem of having to decide between his country and his emotions, while patriotism from the First World War can be seen in Lord Kitchener, the man from the 'Your country needs *you*!' posters. His birthday was the 24th.

Being the face on the poster, the popular image of the age, is something that Cancerians are rather good at. George Michael, born on 25th June, is a good current example. And, of course, the most famous, most photographed woman in the world, the Princess of Wales, is a Cancerian, too, with her birthday on 1st July. One half of the team who designed her wedding dress, Elizabeth Emanuel, isn't far away, on the 5th, while two grand old ladies of Californian society, Barbara Stanwyck and Nancy Reagan, both celebrate on the 6th. They share their birthday with another face from the posters, Sylvester Stallone (and his ex-wife, Brigitte Nielsen, is yet another Cancerian — 15th July). America itself has its birthday on the Fourth of July, of course, and so did its 29th president, Calvin Coolidge.

Dr David Owen, founder, leader and survivor of the Social Democrats, has his birthday on 2nd July, while the 3rd is reserved for two Toms: Stoppard the playwright, and Cruise the star of *Top Gun*.

Daring feats of aviation don't sound quite right for the careful Cancerian, but Amy Johnson's birthday was the same as the Princess of Wales', while Count Zeppelin, builder of the airships which bore his name, had his birthday a week later, on the 8th. Another Cancerian balloonist, Richard Branson, celebrates on the 18th, while another millionaire, John D. Rockefeller (yes, that one) was born on the 9th, which is also Ted Heath's birthday.

The middle week of July seems full of Hollywood greats. Yul Brynner was born on the 11th, Harrison Ford on the 13th, Ginger Rogers' birthday is the 16th, and the great James Cagney comes a day later on the 17th. A famous *real* gangster, 'Legs' Diamond, was born on 10th July.

Well-loved faces from television can also be Cancerians. Christopher Quinten, formerly from *Coronation Street,* and Sir Alastair Burnet share a birthday on 13th July, while Ken Kercheval, who plays the long-suffering Cliff Barnes in *Dallas,* is a few days later on the 15th.

Cancerian women may have firm views, but seldom similar ones. Emmeline Pankhurst, the suffragette, was born on 14th July; romantic novelist Barbara Cartland has her birthday five days earlier on the 9th. Finally, two actresses to end the sign, sharing 20th July: Diana Rigg, and Wendy Richards from *Eastenders*.

LEO

Leo is the sign of the lion, of course, and is also said to be the sign of kings. It's rather fitting, then, to find that Haile Selassie, last king of Ethiopia, and one of whose titles was 'lion of Judah', had his birthday on the first day of Leo, on the 23rd. There hasn't been a Leo king of England for a good while, but Queens and Princesses seem to like the sign; the Queen Mother celebrates her birthday on 4th August, her daughter Princess Margaret on the 21st, and Princess Anne on the 15th.

Leo rulers don't necessarily have to be royal: Mussolini was born on 28th July, and Napoleon on 15th August. Fidel Castro is a Leo, too.

Leo brings things to *prominence*: it makes people stand out, because they are the first, the most, or the only. Louise Brown, the first test-tube baby, is a Leo, born on 25th July, and so is Neil Armstrong, the first man on the Moon. His birthday is 5th August. Steve Davis, the world's finest snooker player, is a late Leo, with his birthday on 22nd August, while Daley Thomson, the world's finest decathlete, comes rather earlier in the sign on 30th July, something he shares with singer Kate Bush. Kate and Daley were born on the same day *in the same year*; it is merely the fact that they were born at different times of day which makes them look dissimilar. See page 206 for how this happens.

July 30th also seems to produce far-sighted industrialists; Henry Ford was born then, and it's Sir Clive Sinclair's birthday, too. Nor is the day exhausted; it's Emily Brontë's birthday, as well.

Literary Leos are plentiful. Poet Robert Graves shared 24th July with Alexandre Dumas, the creator of the *Three Musketeers*, while his compatriot Guy de Maupassant, master of the short story, was born on 5th August, one day before Tennyson's birthday. The day before Maupassant, the 4th, was Shelley's birthday, and one day before *that* gets you Rupert Brooke, who wrote of 'some corner of a foreign field That is forever England'.

Literary lions must also include George Bernard Shaw, born on 26th July. The 26th seems to be another powerful date, like the 30th, because along with Shaw we find Carl Jung, the pioneering psychoanalyst; Stanley Kubrick, the director of films like *2001*, *A Clockwork Orange* and *Full Metal Jacket*; and Mick Jagger.

There are more film directors and rock stars in the sign, too, and some of them even share birthdays; Cecil B. deMille was born on 12th August, and so was Mark Knopfler of 'Dire Straits'.

Leo film stars are plentiful. Among the best known are Dustin Hoffman, on 8th August, Robert de Niro on the 17th, and Robert Redford on the following day.

Around the same part of the sign come Madonna and Sean Penn, whose birthdays are just one day apart on the 16th and 17th respectively.

Leo also seems to have produced star interviewers — people who are sometimes more famous than the people they talk to. Terry Wogan has his birthday on 3rd August, the day after Alan Whicker's birthday, while Barry Norman brings up the rear on the 21st. Nor should it be forgotten that television's inventor, John Logie Baird, was a Leo too: 13th August.

Then there are those whose singularity, their 'one-and-only'-ness, could only come from Leo: Mata Hari and Andy Warhol, a day apart on 7th and 8th August; and Lawrence of Arabia, a clear indication of how Leos are at their best when they can do things their own way, on 15th August.

Finally, on the last day of the sign, a fine example of the energy, confidence, and star quality which is the sign at its best: Gene Kelly. Only a Leo can sing in the rain.

Virgo

Virgo is the sign of the Virgin, or young woman, and when Queen Elizabeth was called the Virgin Queen the reference was to her horoscope as well as her unmarried status: she was born right in the middle of the sign, on 7 September. More recently, though, it doesn't seem to have been the sign of the royals so much as the sign of royal *husbands*; Mark Phillips is a 22 September Virgo, Princess Alexandra's husband Angus Ogilvy celebrates just over a week earlier, on the 14th, and the co-founder of the current royal dynasty, Queen Victoria's consort Prince Albert, was an early Virgo with his birthday on 26 August. The most recent royal Virgo is Prince Harry, born on 15 September.

Virgo is the sign of those who have an eye for detail, as you probably know by now. It's not surprising, then, to find Frederick Forsyth, author of *The Day of the Jackal*, celebrating his birthday on 25 August. He's only one day before an earlier writer of adventure stories, John Buchan.

Virgoan authors seem to be quite plentiful, probably because the sign is governed by the planet Mercury, which also looks after all forms of words and communication. Nor are they limited to thrillers: D. H. Lawrence was born on 11 September, Mary Shelley, who wrote *Frankenstein*, was born on 28 August, and for those who like a really long read, then Tolstoy the author of *War and Peace*, was born on the 26th. Agatha Christie was a Virgo too, born on the 15th, and so was H. G.Wells, down at the end of the sign on the 21st.

Wells, who wrote, among other things, *The War of the Worlds*, about an invasion from Mars, shares his birthday with Gustav Holst, the composer of the 'Planets' suite. Interesting, isn't it?

Classical music enthusiasts may like to note that as well as Holst's, Bruckner's birthday is in Virgo, on the 4th — but pop music fans will prefer to move on a day to the 5th, which is the birthday of Freddie Mercury from Queen. Two days further on reaches Buddy Holly's birthday on the 7th, while two days further on again finds Eurythmic Dave Stewart, on the 9th. Nor should we forget Michael Jackson, an early Virgo from 29 August.

Hollywood has its share of Virgoan greats, of course, including Sam Goldwyn himself, of Metro-Goldwyn-Mayer fame, who was born on the 27th. Two days before him, on the 25th, is Sean Connery, while two days after him comes Richard Gere.

Raquel Welch is a Virgo; 5 September, a date she shares with the late Russell Harty, both one day after the birthday of the outlaw Jesse James. The queens of the silver screen seem to cluster together at the end of the sign, though, with Lauren Bacall on the 16th, Greta Garbo on the 18th, and Sophia Loren on the 20th. Sophia Loren doesn't really have a typical Virgoan appearance, and neither does Linda Lusardi, whose birthday is the same as Greta Garbo's — the 18th — but Twiggy certainly does, and her birthday falls neatly between the two, on the 19th.

Finally, there's a Virgoan couple in *Dallas*: Linda Gray (Sue Ellen) and Larry Hagman (J.R.) are both from the sign — she's the 12th, and he's the 21st of September.

LIBRA

Libra is the sign most usually connected to the Arts and Music, but there is an emphasis on being visually attractive, too; Librans are often very beautiful, and this, in combination with their personal charm, enables them to get away with things that the other eleven signs couldn't hope to.

Libran composers are interesting. Most of them come from this century, and their music seems to evoke a certain *visual* style, a particular image, as well as a musical style; George Gershwin is a good example. He was born on 26th September, the same day as Bryan Ferry, another musician with a distinct visual style. Their birthday comes just two days after the birthday of F. Scott Fitzgerald, author of *The Great Gatsby*, and of course Gershwin's music and Fitzgerald's writing form a perfect Libran match for each other since they were produced at about the same time.

The few days around 25th September seem to be an eternal source of artistic talent; the great actress Sarah Bernhardt was born on the 24th, and the poet T. S. Eliot on the 25th. There are more musical

Librans, too: the composer Saint-Saëns was born on 9th October, a date he shares with John Lennon, whereas the next day, the 10th, was Guiseppe Verdi's birthday.

Sporting Librans aren't hard to find, either, showing that grace of movement that is built into the sign; Sebastian Coe is a 29th September Libran, while his great rival Steve Ovett is just ten days later on 9th October. The great Libran sport, however, must be tennis, which is not only played with two people (or even better, two pairs), but which has a pleasing back-and-forth rhythm which appeals to the Libran mind. The legendary Helen Wills was born on 6th October, while the game's most successful female player in the modern era, Martina Navratilova, celebrates on the 18th.

Libran politicians are surprisingly common; perhaps they like the to-and-fro of political argument, Mrs Thatcher has her birthday on 13th October, just one day before the birthday of Eamon de Valera, who was the first leader of the state of Eire, the juxtaposition is thought-provoking.

More Libran politicians include former U.S. President Jimmy Carter, whose birthday is 1st October, the day before that of Mahatma Gandhi, India's greatest leader. A little while later, on the 10th, comes South African Paul Kruger, who gave his name to the gold coin, the Krugerrand.

The early days of October also seem to produce artists and designers, and art critics, too. The painter J. F. Millet shares 4th October with Sir Terence Conran, but hot on their heels come Melvyn Bragg and Clive James, whose birthdays are on the 6th and 7th respectively. Two playwrights sit back to back in the middle of the month; Eugene O'Neill on the 16th, and Oscar Wilde on the 15th. The 15th seems to be an extraordinary day — is also the birthday of the philosopher Nietzsche, and that of Sarah, the Duchess of York. Some of Nietzsche's ideas found favour with Heinrich Himmler, whose birthday was just over a week earlier, on the 7th.

Two days further back is the 5th, and that's Bob Geldof's birthday. Librans like supporting worthy causes — it helps restore the *balance* of things — which is why Brigitte Bardot, whose birthday is 28th September, works so hard for animal charities.

To end the sign with a flourish, there's another famous French Libran beauty, Catherine Deneuve, and a suitably romantic Libran composer/performer, Franz Liszt. They share 22nd October.

SCORPIO

Traditionally, Scorpios have always been said to have a passionate, almost mesmerizing force of personality. Richard Burton seemed always to be full of the intensity of his sign, and his birthday was on 10th November. Whether Count Dracula was a Scorpio isn't known — his appearance and activities are certainly suggestive of the sign — but his creator, Bram Stoker, certainly was, with his birthday just a couple of days before Burton's, on the 8th. In between them, on the 9th, comes King Edward VII, Queen Victoria's son, and the king who gave his name to the era he lived in. The Scorpio influence seems to have stayed in his descendants down the generations: Prince Charles's birthday is 14th November, and Charles's nephew Peter Phillips is only a day later (the 15th), while his cousin Viscount Linley comes a little earlier in the sign, on the 3rd.

Political astrologers often see a link between the sign of Scorpio and the extreme right in politics: one link which is easy to spot is their use of the Scorpionic colours, black and red. Sir Oswald Mosley was a Scorpio (16th November), but a better example of a

Scorpio's liking for *hidden power* is Josef Goebbels, born on 29th October.

Scorpio political leaders are quite easy to find: their determination to succeed helps them reach the top. Many of them, though, were or are revolutionaries for their time, in that their views were those which went against the prevailing mood, or came to power through violent acts, which are a feature of the sign. Russian revolutionary Trotsky was a 7th November Scorpio; Sun Yat-Sen, who overthrew the last Chinese emperor, was born on 12th November; and American president Theodore Roosevelt, a 27th October Scorpio who gave his name to the teddy bear, came to power because his predecessor was assassinated. Current leaders include Francois Mitterand, whose birthday is a day before Roosevelt's.

That same pair of birthdays — the 26th and 27th of October — belong to Bob Hoskins and John Cleese respectively, though two more different-looking individuals would be hard to imagine.

Scorpios are supposedly too busy to give their time to writing, but despite that the sign has produced quite a few literary names. The playwright Sheridan, born on 30th October, had the same birthday as one of this century's most enigmatic poets, Ezra Pound. The grandfather of English literature, Chaucer, was a Scorpio, too (25th October), while at the end of the sign, on 22nd November, we find George Eliot, who was really Mary Evans, of course: a typical piece of Scorpionic subterfuge!

Penetrating mysteries, digging into things, is something Scorpios are good at, and for that there is no better example than Marie Curie, radium's discoverer, who shares Trotsky's birthday, the 7th. Determination to get there in another field characterizes the polar explorer Richard Byrd, an early Scorpio from the 25th. A different sort of mystery is found in the books of Dick

Francis, whose birthday is 31st October. Horses are actually supposed to be Sagittarian, but there is another champion jockey who is a Scorpio: Lester Piggott, born on 5th November.

Pop music seems to span the sign neatly: right at the beginning, on 24th October, Rolling Stone Bill Wyman celebrates, while at the other end, Kim Wilde and Jonathan Ross are separated by just one day; they were born on 17th and 18th November, respectively, in the same year — 1960. Astrology says that they should be *very* similar indeed, in personality and opinions, if not in looks.

Finally, two champions in their sports. Frank Bruno celebrates on the 16th, while at the very end of the sign, the 22nd, comes tennis star Billie Jean King, a real illustration of the concentration and determination to succeed which makes the sign so memorable.

SAGITTARIUS

There's a zesty, vivid quality about Sagittarians. Larger and frequently louder, than most people, they have a unique combination of energy and optimism which enables them to get away with things that the other eleven signs can only dream of.

This swashbuckling quality found itself perfectly expressed in Hollywood by Douglas Fairbanks Jr, whose birthday is 9th December. He shares his birthday with another heroic leading man from the movies, Kirk Douglas. Other Sagittarians from the great day of the movies include Boris Karloff, the original Frankenstein's monster, born right at the beginning of the sign on 23rd November, and Edward G. Robinson, who was born on 12th December. His birthday is also that of Frank Sinatra, whose tremendous talent combines with a strong sense of independence in a way which is entirely typical of the sign. Jane Fonda, whose birthday is 21st December, has these qualities, too.

A similar confidence in his own abilities can be seen in Ian Botham, born on 24th November, while the Sagittarian's ability to bounce back from misfortune is well demonstrated by Tina Turner, who is two days later, on the 26th. Rolling Stone Keith Richards is a Sagittarian, too — 18th December is his birthday.

Sometimes Sagittarian behaviour goes beyond what some people think reasonable. Jonathan King and Bette Midler are both from the sign: her birthday is the 1st, and his the 6th.

The sharp way with words which they both have is a particular Sagittarian ability, and there are many who have become famous for it. Billy Connolly is another good example, sharing Ian Botham's birthday on the 24th, but there's also Noel Coward, whose birthday was the 16th, and the remarkable 'double' of Mark Twain, the first author to use a typewriter (a forward-thinking Sagittarian), and Jonathan Swift, the satirist author of *Gulliver's Travels*. Twain and Swift were both born on 30th November.

30th November was also Churchill's birthday. He is just one of a number of important world figures who had a major part to play in the Second World War. General de Gaulle was a Sagittarian from 22nd November, right at the start of the sign. The Spanish dictator General Franco was born on 4th December, while the King of England at the time, George VI, had his birthday on the 14th — and his younger brother the Duke of Kent was a Sagittarian too, on the 20th.

Vision and imagination, coupled with a sense of wonderment, are an essential part of every Sagittarian. Two Sagittarians whose imagination has delighted millions are Walt Disney, whose birthday was 5th December, and Steven Spielberg, who celebrates on the 18th. Earlier imaginative Sagittarians had to rely on painting and poetry to communicate their ideas: William Blake's birthday was 30th November, while Christina Rosetti's was 5th December. A different sort of imagination is shown by Charles Schulz (26th November), creator of the *Peanuts* cartoons; their penetrating yet kindly insight into the way we all feel is very Sagittarian.

Finally, two Sagittarians whose vision extends even into the far future: the seer Nostradamus, born on 14th December, and Arthur C. Clarke, whose birthday is two days later on the 16th.

CAPRICORN

Capricorns are known for their belief in hard work and duty. These sentiments are sometimes called 'Victorian values', and it is no surprise to note that the great Prime Minister Gladstone was a Capricorn, born on 29th December. It is worth noting that Disraeli, born eight days earlier on the 21st, was actually a late Sagittarian; page 194 will show you why they didn't agree.

Other Capricorn politicians all show those typical Capricorn qualities of hardness and endurance. A day before Gladstone comes Woodrow Wilson, the US president whose administration introduced the prohibition of alcohol, while four days later comes Russian leader Josef Stalin (on 2nd January, probably — the date is uncertain). A little earlier in the sign, on 26th December, comes Mao Tse-Tung, the Chinese revolutionary leader. Finally, at the other end of the sign, there is the great Liberal leader David Lloyd George, whose birthday was on 17th January.

There is more to Capricorn than politicians, though. There are inventors, too, like Sir Isaac Pitman, shorthand's creator, born on 4th January, and millionaire recluse Howard Hughes, who comes at the beginning of the sign on 23rd December. Both of them were concerned with making better use of the time available — a very Capricornian idea. Capricorn pioneers whose lasting fame comes from humanitarian rather than commercial enterprises include Louis Pasteur, born on December 27th, and Clara Barton, the founder of the Red Cross, who was born on Christmas Day. Christmas Day was also Isaac Newton's birthday: only a Capricorn, with his interest in matters of weight, and keeping to the rules, could formulate laws of motion and gravity.

Old folk tales say that those born on New Year's Day can more or less do what they wish with life: it is they who give the orders. J. Edgar Hoover, founder of the FBI, was born then.

Literary and artistic Capricorns are a little hard to find: most of them prefer politics to painting. Despite that, though, there is Kipling, born on 30th December. *The Hobbit*'s creator J. R. R. Tolkien on 4th January, and at the other end of the sign, Cézanne, on the 19th. Capricorn's acutely observed but rather dry humour may be showing itself as Rowan Atkinson's career develops. His birthday is 6th January.

Capricorn women have a cold, rather forbidding beauty, it is said, and with the fine bone structure the sign gives to the face, their good looks seem to last. Marlene Dietrich is perhaps the most extreme form of the Capricorn woman; all the clothes associated with her most memorable film roles are Capricornian in style. Her birthday is 27th December. As a contrast, consider a Royal Capricorn, Princess Michael of Kent, whose birthday is 15th January, and *Dallas* actress Victoria Principal, whose birthday is the 3rd. The previous day, the 2nd, is the birthday of someone who has become famous for photographing the beautiful women of his era, David Bailey.

A good example of a modern Capricorn woman, whose performances have that tough, hard quality which is unique to the sign, is Annie Lennox of the Eurythmics: she is another Christmas Day Capricorn.

Pop music seems to like Capricorns; is it because they have the determination to succeed in a difficult business, or that their rather angular features photograph well? Possibly both. Anyway, besides Annie Lennox, there is David Bowie, born on 8th January, along with Elvis Presley of course, Rod Stewart, two days later on the 10th, and Paul Young a week after that on the 17th.

AQUARIUS

Aquarius is supposed to be the sign most closely connected to science and technology, so it's no surprise to find that Thomas Edison, inventor of almost everything from the phonograph to the light bulb, was an Aquarian. His birthday was February 11th. That puts him just one day away from Charles Darwin on the 12th, whose theories of evolution changed our views about our origins, and four days away from Galileo on the 15th, whose discoveries with the telescope confirmed that the Earth really does orbit the Sun.

Aquarians are always ready to go further than anyone else: The Antarctic explorer Shackleton shared Galileo's birthday on the 15th. Charles Lindbergh, the first man to fly the Atlantic solo, was an Aquarian, with his birthday on February 4th; and so was Sir Henry Stanley, the man who found Dr Livingstone — his birthday was on January 28th.

There seems to be a definite connection between US presidents and Aquarius. Ronald Reagan's birthday is February 6th, which puts him neatly in the middle of the sign, one week earlier than Abraham Lincoln, who was born on the 12th, and one week later than Franklin D. Roosevelt, who was born on January 30th. The day before that — the 29th — was also the birthday of McKinley, who was the US president assassinated in 1901.

Literary Aquarians are plentiful, and they seem to cluster together around certain dates. Virginia Woolf and Somerset Maugham, for example, shared January 25th as their birthday, while a little later on in the sign Charles Dickens, born on February 7th, is just in front of John Ruskin, born on the 8th.

Sharing Ruskin's birthday is Jules Verne, who was a forward-looking Aquarian author if ever there was one — the grandfather of science fiction, Aquarius' favourite sort of reading. A different sort of fantastic writing can be found in the works of Lewis Carroll, *Alice in Wonderland*'s author, who was born on January 27th, which was also Mozart's birthday. Aquarius is one of the more musical signs, by the way; Yehudi Menuhin's birthday is on January 22nd.

One day before Lewis Carroll and Mozart is Paul Newman's birthday, on the 26th. Newman is an example of the distinctive cool blue-eyed blond look which many Aquarians have. Interestingly, two actresses famous for their glamorous, but nonetheless Aquarian, good looks have birthdays only a day apart — Farrah Fawcett and Morgan Fairchild, from February 2nd and 3rd respectively. February 2nd was Nell Gwynne's birthday, too, so perhaps there is something about the date which produces the pin-up faces for an era.

Independence is the strongest Aquarian character trait, and it can be seen quite clearly in people like feminist writer Germaine Greer, who was born on January 29th, in Princess Caroline of Monaco, born on the 23rd, and in tennis player John McEnroe, who is at the other end of the sign on the 16th. The cinema's most famous rebel, James Dean, comes somewhere between them, on the 8th. Clark Gable, possibly the cinema's most famous leading man, was also an Aquarian: February 1st, in fact.

Finally, an organization — CND, the Campaign for Nuclear Disarmament. This highly Aquarian cause was started on February 18th, which just brings it into the end of the sign.

PISCES

Pisces is probably the most artistic of the signs, and can offer a wider range of poets, musicians, and artists than any other. To begin with, two dancers; the legendary Vaslav Nijinsky was born on February 28th, while Rudolf Nureyev's birthday is at the other end of the sign on March 17th. His birthday is a day before that of composer Rimsky-Korsakov, on the 18th, which is in turn a fortnight after Vivaldi's, on the 4th. Chopin was a Piscean, too; his birthday was February 22nd.

February 22nd seems to have produced some remarkable people. Besides Chopin, it also produced Lord Baden-Powell, founder of the Scout movement, and George Washington, the first president of the United States. Finally, February 22nd was the birthday of one of the best-known entries in the *Guinness Book of Records* — Robert Wadlow, the tallest man ever.

It is also the birthday of the Duchess of Kent, just one of a number of the present Royal Family who are Pisceans; The Earl of Snowdon's birthday is March 7th, Prince Edward's is three days later on the 10th, and right at the beginning of the sign, on the 19th of February, is Prince Andrew. Andrew is an interesting example of being 'on the cusp' (see page 243). The Sun entered Pisces at 3.26 pm on February 19th, 1960, and he was born at 3.30, four minutes later. He is a very early Pisces but he's still a Pisces. Note, too, how Piscean interests like photography and the theatre show up in the Royal Family here.

Amongst famous Piscean writers are Victor Hugo, author of *Les Miserables*, who was born on February 26th; poetess Elizabeth Barrett Browning on March 6th, and Kenneth Grahame, author of the children's favourite *Wind in the Willows*, on the 8th. Elizabeth Barrett Browning shares her birthday with Michaelangelo, the great painter and sculptor.

A different sort of writing is shown by the science-fiction works of L. Ron Hubbard, a March 13th Piscean. Hubbard was also the founder of the Church of Scientology, of course. Fellow Piscean William Bramwell Booth (another March 8th birthday), founder of the Salvation Army, might have been surprised. Hubbard shares his birthday with Percival Lowell, an astronomer whose work led to the discovery of Pluto. Another Piscean astronomer, Patrick Moore, has his birthday on March 4th.

Albert Einstein was a Piscean, too, born on March 14th. His birthday is shared by Michael Caine, which not many people know. Nor do they know that Sir Henry Wood, in whose memory the 'Prom' concerts are held each summer had the same birthday as Alexander Graham Bell, the inventor of the telephone. The date in question is March 3rd.

There are more Piscean politicians than might be expected for this most impressionable and emotional of signs. Harold Wilson's birthday is March 11th (a date he shares with Rupert Murdoch, the newspaper magnate), while Neville Chamberlain, Prime Minister of the 1930's, had his birthday on the 18th. Mikhail Gorbachev, Russia's newest leader, celebrates on March 2nd.

Finally, a neat piece of astrological coincidence. Since Roman times, or even before that, the end of the sign of

Pisces has been associated with prisons. At the very end of the sign, on March 19th, comes the birthday of Patrick McGoohan — *The Prisoner*.

8
ALL THE SAME BUT DIFFERENT

One of the questions that astrologers usually get asked is that if everybody is different and unique and individual, how can all the people in the world from one Sun sign be the same?

The answer is that everyone from each of the twelve Sun signs has just one thing in common — their Sun sign. They each have many other things about them, however, which are *not* shared by everyone else, and that's what makes them all different.

When an astrologer draws a chart for a single individual, he looks at the position in the sky not just of the Sun, but of all the other planets as well, from Mercury out to Pluto. Just because the Sun may be in Libra doesn't mean that the other planets will be: as I write this, in late 1988, Jupiter is in Gemini and Saturn is in Sagittarius, for example. This means that someone born in October might well think of themselves as a Libran, because of the Sun's position, but there are also going to be parts of them which are like a Gemini or a Sagittarian, or whatever.

This happens because the planets don't go round the zodiac at the same speed as the Sun. Some of them stay for months, or even years, in the same sign, while at the other extreme the Moon goes round the whole twelve signs in just under a month, changing signs every two and a half days.

It would be just as true to say that all the people born

when Venus was in Capricorn have something in common with each other as it is to say that all the people born with the Sun in Taurus have, but it's very unlikely that you'll ever see horoscopes in magazines for such people to read, and for two good reasons.

Firstly, the Sun's motions are linked to the calendar: each year on a given date the Sun is more or less in the same part of the zodiac, so as long as you know your birthday, you know which sign the Sun is in. Venus's motion doesn't match the calendar at all, and so the magazines and newspapers would have to print large lists to say that Venus was in this sign on this date in this year, and so on, which is all very inconvenient.

Secondly, the Sun is the strongest influence, astrologically. To show what you are according to your Sun sign describes the main part of your personality, whereas to describe what you are according to your Venus sign of Mars sign only shows a little bit. An important bit, sure, but not as central as the Sun sign description.

Only when *all* the planets' influences are taken into account does the full picture emerge. It is this, the combination of all the planets in all their various signs, and the parts of the sky they occupy at the moment of your birth, and at the place of your birth, which makes up a horoscope, and each one is different. The number of combinations is far from twelve, or even twelve times twelve; the answer is in billions of billions, more than enough for every person who ever lived to have a different horoscope, and to last us for a million years to come.

Mind-boggling thought, isn't it? They are all different, and yet because so many of them share common elements, such as the Sun in a particular sign, they are to some extent the same.

Something that isn't done very often, but which is quite an eye-opener, is to have a look at the groups of people who have the slow-moving planets in the same sign. Take Uranus as an example: it takes seven years for it to pass through just one sign of the zodiac, and so every single person born during that time, no matter where, or no matter what their Sun sign, will have Uranus's influence in the same sign, and so have something in common with everyone else born during that time.

You may be wondering what it is that you have in common with everybody else born within a few years of you, since you all look different and do different things, but what links you all together is something bigger than that. What we're labelling here is *generations*. Here are the children of the Depression, the Baby Boomers, the Rock 'n' Rollers, the Hippies — generations with their own particular styles and beliefs. This is why tastes change every few years. What happens is that a new group of people come to maturity who were born at a time when the outer planets were in another sign.

On the next page there is a graph which shows you how the big planets moved through the zodiac in the middle years of this century. Have a look to see where they were when you were born. Have a look for somebody who is a few years younger than you, and who appears to represent a different generation. You will see that the planets have changed signs. Now have a look for the year when an older relative, perhaps your mother or father, was born. The difference between your planetary placings and theirs is the zodiacal version of the generation gap, and it shows why your tastes in, say, music, are so different from those of an older person, even if your Sun signs are the same. These outer planet positions are the things which really 'date' us, no matter how hard we try to keep up!

Here's a quick guide to what was when, for use with the graph.

Pre – 1938: Neptune in Virgo and Pluto in Cancer for

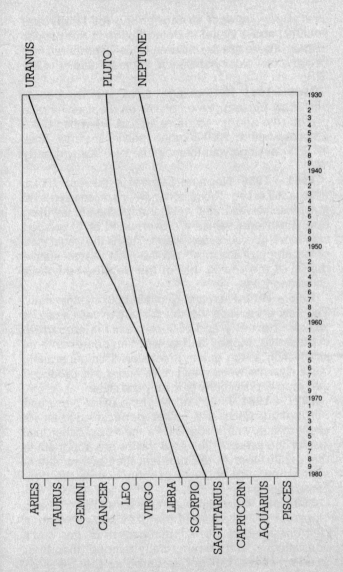

everybody gives a strong feeling for family and country, and a belief in doing things in the proper manner. These are the children of the Depression, who become the 'older generation' to the teenagers of the '60s.

1938 – 1941: Pluto changes signs, into Leo. People born now place more emphasis on themselves than previously, and try to rebel against what has been accepted before. As this group reaches maturity, Rock 'n' Roll develops with them, in the late '50s and early '60s.

1941 – 1956: Neptune changes signs, into Libra; Pluto is still in Leo. Those born now are more interested in themselves and their relationships than in anything else. Traditional values are overturned and replaced with more liberal, 'softer' views. This is the generation of the hippy philosophy, and the most representative music of the era is that of the Beatles and their contemporaries.

1956 – 1971: Pluto and Neptune both change signs. The new generation has much sharper values, and a streak of cruelty and ruthlessness which can be destructive. Money and power replace emotional satisfaction as the guiding ambition. This generation, currently in its twenties and early thirties, has produced the 'yuppie' philosophy of money and status.

1971 – 1984: Pluto and Neptune enter Libra and Sagittarius. This is a softer generation than its predecessor, with a concern for the future rather than just for the present. Religious values are important to this group, too. At the moment they are mostly at school, but will come to prominence as the next century opens.

1984 on: Pluto and Neptune enter Scorpio and Capricorn. The plans of the previous generation become reality here; this group is far more constructive, and commercially minded, than their predecessors, but not as harsh as the '56 – '71 generation. Great reforms in international politics and financing will take place when this generation, currently small children, grows to maturity.

As Uranus changes signs more frequently than the slower pair of Neptune and Pluto, you can use it to mark off different sub-sections within the generations. Sometimes just a difference of a single year in dates of birth can make all the difference between the values and beliefs of two people from similar background, or even from the same family. Try it and see!

9
QUICK FACTS
ABOUT YOU

The following pages provide a quick summary of some
Sun sign trivia — all the bits and pieces relevant to
people born under each sign.

ARIES

Best Qualities: Directness, Initiative, Energy

Worst Qualities: Impatience, Self-centredness, Aggressiveness

Best Match: Aquarius

Worst Match: Taurus

Favourite Weakness: Fast cars

Best Day: Tuesday

Worst Day: Friday

Lucky Numbers: 1, 5

Colour: Red

Birthstones: Ruby, Diamond

Trees: Thorn, Chestnut

Flower: Thistle

Vegetables: Onion, Radish

Metals: Iron, Steel

TAURUS

Best Qualities: Patience, Determination, Endurance

Worst Qualities: Stubbornness, Greediness, Possessiveness

Best Match: Cancer

Worst Match: Aries

Favourite Weakness: Food

Best Day: Friday

Worst Day: Tuesday

Lucky Numbers: 2, 7

Colours: Green, Pink

Birthstones: Emerald, Topaz

Trees: Sycamore, Apple

Flowers: Rose, Lily

Fruits: Apple, Peach

Metal: Copper

GEMINI

Best Qualities: Mental agility, Flexibility, Communicative nature

Worst Qualities: Changeability, Lack of sympathy, Decietfulness

Best Match: Leo

Worst Match: Pisces

Favourite Weakness: Gambling

Best Day: Wednesday

Worst Day: Friday

Lucky Numbers: 3, 8

Colours: Yellow, all multicolour mixtures, checks

Birthstones: Agate, Marcasite

Tree: Walnut

Flower: Lavender

Herbs: Caraway seed, Marjoram

Metal: Mercury

CANCER

Best Qualities: Sympathy, Protectiveness, Dependability

Worst Qualities: Touchiness, Possessiveness, Inability to take objective view

Best Match: Taurus

Worst Match: Gemini

Favourite Weakness: Worrying about things

Best Day: Monday

Worst Day: Wednesday

Lucky Numbers: 4, 9

Colours: White, Silver, all pearlescent finishes

Birthstones: Pearl, Moonstone

Tree: Willow

Flowers: Lily, White rose

Vegetables: Cabbage, Lettuce

Metal: Silver

LEO

Best Qualities: Zest for life, Generosity, Ability to organize and lead

Worst Qualities: Pride, Extravagance, Selfcentredness

Best Match: Aries

Worst Match: Capricorn

Favourite Weakness: Playing to the crowd

Best Day: Sunday

Worst Day: Saturday

Lucky Numbers: 5, 6, 1

Colours: Gold, Rich reds and purples, Royal colours

Birthstone: Diamond

Tree: Ash

Flowers: Poppy, Marigold

Fruits: All citrus fruits

Metal: Gold

VIRGO

Best Qualities: Patience, Perception, Talent for skilled work

Worst Qualities: Fault-finding, Narrow-mindedness, Intolerance

Best Match: Cancer

Worst Match: Libra

Favourite Weakness: Self-punishment

Best Day: Wednesday

Worst Day: Thursday

Lucky Numbers: 6, 8

Colours: Navy blue, Muted greens, Grey

Birthstones: Green onyx

Tree: Hazel

Flowers: Azalea, Lily of the Valley

Herbs: Parsley, Marjoram, Caraway, Dill

Metal: Quicksilver

LIBRA

Best Qualities: Friendliness, Fairness, Gracefulness

Worst Qualities: Indecisiveness, Lack of staying power, Laziness

Best Match: Sagittarius

Worst Match: Virgo

Favourite Weakness: Romance

Best Day: Friday

Worst Day: Wednesday

Lucky Number: 7

Colours: Sky blue, Leaf green, Pink

Birthstone: Sapphire

Trees: Ash, Cypress

Flowers: Lily, Foxglove, Violet

Herb: Mint

Metal: Copper

SCORPIO

Best Qualities: Willpower, Self-control, Ability to survive setbacks

Worst Qualities: Inflexibility, Ruthlessness, Suspicious mind

Best Match: Capricorn

Worst Match: Libra

Favourite Weakness: Self-destuction

Best Day: Tuesday

Worst Day: Friday

Lucky Numbers: 8, 5

Colours: Red, Black

Birthstones: Jasper, Beryl

Tree: Blackthorn

Flowers: Thistle, Honeysuckle

Herbs: Basil, Cress

Metals: Iron, Steel

SAGITTARIUS

Best Qualities: Intelligence, Optimism, Honesty

Worst Qualities: Carelessness, Tactlessness, Trusting to luck

Best Match: Libra

Worst Match: Capricorn

Favourite Weakness: Travelling

Best Day: Thursday

Worst Day: Saturday

Lucky Numbers: 9, 4, 3

Colours: Deep blue, Purple

Birthstones: Amethyst, Zircon

Tree: Oak

Flowers: Dandelions, Violet

Spices: Cloves, Nutmeg

Metals: Tin, Pewter

CAPRICORN

Best Qualities: Capacity for hard work, Endurance, Sense of duty

Worst Qualities: Seriousness, Meanness, Lack of imagination

Best Match: Scorpio

Worst Match: Sagittarius

Favourite Weakness: Status symbols

Best Day: Saturday

Worst Day: Thursday

Lucky Numbers: 10, 3, 4

Colours: Black, Grey, Dark green

Birthstones: Onyx, Lapis lazuli

Trees: Willow, Yew

Flowers: Poppy, Nightshade

Herb: Sage

Metal: Lead

AQUARIUS

Best Qualities: Friendliness, Independance, Clear thinking

Worst Qualities: Emotional coolness, Eccentricity, Dislike of authority

Best Match: Libra

Worst Match: Cancer

Favourite Weakness: 'Logical' reasons

Best Day: Saturday

Worst Day: Monday

Lucky Numbers: 11, 3, 4

Colours: Grey, Indigo, Electric blue

Birthstones: Chalcedony, Lapis lazuli

Trees: Willow, Yew

Flowers: Poppy, Nightshade

Herb: Sage

Metal: Lead

PISCES

Best Qualities: Imagination, Sensitivity, Easy-going

Worst Qualities: Impressionability, Indecisiveness, Lack of willpower or endurance

Best Match: Cancer

Worst Match: Aries

Favourite Weakness: Escaping decisions

Best Day: Thursday

Worst Day: Wednesday

Lucky Numbers: 12, 4, 3

Colours: Purple, Turquoise, Greeny-blues

Birthstones: Amethyst, Opal, Turquoise

Trees: Ash, Lime

Flowers: Water-lily, Samphire

Herbs: Cloves, Nutmeg

Metals: Tin, Pewter

POSTSCRIPT

If you enjoyed finding out about your lifestyle, your relationships, and your appearance, and you would like to go a little deeper into yourself, you might like to read *The Complete Sun Sign Guide*, also from the Aquarian Press. It shows you the twelve signs from the inside rather than the outside, and explains *why* you act the way you do, what you're aiming for, how you handle other people, and how they handle you. It also explains why the zodiac has twelve signs, and how you fit into it all: a book with not just the answers, but the reasons as well.